ADVANCE PRAISE
FOR TRANSFLUENCE

"Walt Rakowich knows the challenges of leading a cultural transformation in a global recession and hard times. His insights and experience are perfect for helping leaders who will take us all into a better future. If you need a vision of the way forward, this book is your roadmap."

- CHESTER ELTON, bestselling author of *All In*, *The Carrot Principle*, and *Leading with Gratitude*

"*Transfluence* dives into the work of inner leadership, a process all leaders need before they can effectively empower others. Honesty, humility, and heart, the author's 3H-Core principles, are needed today more than ever before. This is a must-read for every aspiring leader."

- SUSAN PACKARD, former COO of HGTV and author of *New Rules of the Game* and *Fully Human*

"Trust is the cornerstone of great leadership. And *Transfluence* provides a proven approach to building trust in the challenging climates of the modern marketplace. This book is a must-read no matter where you are in your leadership journey."

- JOEL PETERSON, chairman of JetBlue Airways and the founding partner of Peterson Partners

"Two sad days in my life: When I was ten years old and found out Santa Claus was not real. And when I was fifty years old and found out that many CEOs, business experts, and leadership authors were just like Santa Claus—not real. And then there are the Walt Rakowiches of the world. The 200-plus pages in this book will change the way you love and lead. And if you finish every page, it will also change the lives of all those who choose to follow you."

- TOMMY SPAULDING, *New York Times* bestselling author of *The Heart-Led Leader* and *It's Not Just Who You Know*

"Walt Rakowich is an unsung business leader who successfully rescued his company from the havoc of the Great Financial Crisis. For many years, I have served with Walt as a corporate director and can attest to his exceptional, transformative leadership skills. I highly recommend this inspirational book."

- SHEILA BAIR, chair, FDIC, 2006-2011

"So many books on leadership are actually guides to management. Not only is *Transfluence* an exception, it is noteworthy by connecting leadership to the very essence of human nature."

- ERIC J. BARRON, president, The Pennsylvania State University

TRANSFLUENCE

HOW TO LEAD WITH
TRANSFORMATIVE INFLUENCE
IN TODAY'S CLIMATES OF CHANGE

WALT RAKOWICH

Post Hill
PRESS

A POST HILL PRESS BOOK

ISBN: 978-1-64293-617-9

ISBN (eBook): 978-1-64293-618-6

Transfluence:

How to Lead with Transformative Influence in Today's Climates of Change

© 2020 by Walter C. Rakowich

All Rights Reserved

Cover design by Tony Steck

Post Hill Press

New York • Nashville

posthillpress.com

Published in the United States of America

CONTENTS

FOREWORD

The first time I met Walt Rakowich in person, I fully expected him to pepper me with the usual questions a job candidate gets during a formal interview.

Colorado UpLift, an organization that provides life and leadership mentors to urban youth, was looking for a new CEO, and Walt was (and still is) the chairman of the board. As the former director of the Center for Character and Leadership Development at the United States Air Force Academy, I had a passion for UpLift's mission and had applied for the job.

We met at a small café in Denver in the Fall of 2017, and one of the first things I noticed was that Walt was present. That might not seem like a big deal, or maybe it just seems overly obvious. But what I mean is that he wasn't just physically there, he was fully present. I've interacted with lots of people, especially executives, who were there but not really there, and I knew Walt had a busy schedule. But he wasn't distracted by other priorities or pushing to move quickly so he could go to the next agenda item. Our meeting had his full attention.

The other thing that stood out was that I never felt like it was a job interview. We spent the vast majority of our conversation sketching leadership models on a piece of paper and talking about what great leadership could and should look like. There was excitement in his voice and genuine curiosity in his questions. Instead of an interview, we had a deep, rich conversation about a mutual passion point—leadership.

If it was a test, I guess I passed it, because I was offered the role of CEO. But one of the reasons I took the job was because it was comforting to know the chairman took leadership so seriously. And the more I got to know Walt, the more I found that he doesn't just study great leadership, he models it in ways that add true value to everyone around him.

Ultimately, that's the powerful value of this book. *Transfluence* isn't just another leadership tome, it's an accessible, practical, transferrable approach to what Walt calls "transformative influence" that's based on deep study and a lifetime of rich experiences.

Because I've spent so much of my career studying and teaching leadership, I've grown accustomed to seeing books and articles that underdeliver on this topic. Some give you lots of theory and very few principles you can apply in real-world situations. Some give you application ideas that aren't rooted in substantive theory. Some are based on experiences that were applicable to the writer but add very little transferrable value. Some just rehash what's been written by others for years.

Transfluence offers much more. It builds on the scholarship of others with a unique blending of transformational and servant leadership theories, starting with the essence of leadership and then showing how that applies universally in different situations.

The essence of something is its real, unchanging nature, and there is a nature of leadership that, at its core, is unchanging. Leaders, however, have to take that essence and practice it in a very dynamic world. Walt bridges that gap with an approach that factors in the various climates of leadership.

Who you are will determine how you lead, so Walt provides insights on developing your inner leadership so that the right qualities flow from your heart to the outside world you're trying to lead. The storms of leadership are inevitable, and Walt provides guideposts and actionable advice that will help any leader navigate them, regardless of whether they are internal (things like pride and fear) or external (the circumstances that are constantly changing around you).

The principles and guideposts are grounded in a variety of compelling experiences—everything from what Walt went through as the leader of a global S&P 500 company that faced bankruptcy during the recession to what he learned the summer he worked as a garbageman in Pittsburgh. Some stories are serious and make you pause to think deeply, while others will have you laughing out loud.

In that sense, the book is a manifestation of its message. It's a call to transformative influence that comes from applying your core values, but Walt's experiences also illustrate what the book is suggesting you do. For instance, you'll notice a theme in the pages about the importance of transparency, and Walt shares his fears as a leader in very transparent ways. Honesty, humility, and heart—what Walt calls his 3H-Core—also are clearly evident in every page. You don't just read about what to do, but you see how it was done and learn how to do it yourself so you can develop as a leader.

I've seen Walt model these principles in real life many times since we first met at that café in Denver. I've seen it during difficult board meetings. I've seen it during our one-on-one conversations in my office. And I've seen it in his interactions with others.

One example in particular stands out. Every year we take a group of students who are in the UpLift program on a trip to Tijuana, Mexico, where we help build homes for families in need. Board members like Walt also come and join our staff and the students as we serve and learn together.

One evening after working all day, I was sitting with a group of students who were engaged in a pretty vocal discussion about sports. They weren't unruly, but the trash talk was flowing at a pretty high level when Walt walked in, bypassed the tables that were occupied only with adults, and asked if he could sit with the group.

Frankly, I began wondering how this would go and silently hoping the students would get a clue that it was time to tone things down. They didn't. The smack talk continued, and the next thing you know Walt jumps right in the middle of the conversation. He's firing off his opinions about the best teams and athletes, challenging the opinions of others, and generally interacting just like all the students. He was laughing. The students were laughing. They all were having a great time.

The fact that he made everyone (including himself) feel included in the moment told me a lot about his heart, his humility, and who he was as a person. Walt practices what he teaches regardless of whether he's on the back of a garbage truck, in a board meeting with executives, or sitting with a group of urban teens in Tijuana, Mexico. That's what makes him the perfect person to tell you about *Transfluence*—because his words and his examples will have a transformative influence on your leadership.

– Joseph Sanders, Ph.D.
  Chief Executive Officer, Colorado UpLift
  Retired Colonel and the former director of the Center for Character and
  Leadership Development, United States Air Force Academy

PREFACE

All my plans were disrupted. All of them. The vacation with my wife? On hold. A service project with a nonprofit? Cancelled. Trips to visit our kids? Postponed indefinitely. Board meetings? Welcome to Zoom. A night out for dinner with friends? Maybe next year. Everything had to be reassessed in light of our new reality.

I'm talking about the COVID-19 pandemic in 2020, but here's the interesting reality: I could just as easily be talking about the Great Recession in 2008 or about the terrorists' attacks on September 11, 2001. There were no Zoom meetings and I didn't have to travel to see my kids, but those events also caused huge disruptions in my life, personally and professionally.

When you think about it, history is nothing if not a series of disruptive events. In the last hundred years, for instance, the world has witnessed the Great Depression, the attack on Pearl Harbor and World War II, the Korean and Vietnam wars, the assassinations of Martin Luther King, Jr., and John F. Kennedy, the Iranian hostage standoff, the Gulf War, and the aforementioned recession and terrorist attacks.

The nature of such disruptions might be different, but the essence of great leadership during difficult times remains very much the same. And that's one of the reasons I think you'll find this book particularly relevant to your leadership journey. While it isn't about crisis management, the lessons and principles will resonate with anyone who has led, is leading, or will ever lead during a crisis.

I knew that when I was writing the manuscript, but it really hit home during the first few months of 2020. The year began on a high note. The economy was strong, and this book was in the middle of its production schedule. Editors were editing. Designers were designing the cover and interior pages. Project managers were planning the print run. And marketing and PR firms were preparing to help get the word out. Years of work was coming to fruition when all of a sudden we were introduced to terms like social distancing and self-isolation. Millions of people lost their jobs. Watching the stock market was like watching a rollercoaster at a theme park. And, worst of all, there was a tragic cost in the loss of human lives.

While much of the world hunkered down at home, progress on the book continued on schedule. And soon it became apparent that many of the leaders who would read this book would be dealing with the lasting impacts of a business world reshaped by the pandemic. I suspect you are one of those leaders.

The ironic thing, and this might seem a bit counterintuitive, is that this new reality didn't really impact anything about the content of the book other than prompting me to add this Preface. That's because the biggest difference between leading during a crisis and leading when times are normal is not how we should lead but the fact that others are paying far more attention to how we do lead.

The reality that people are more attuned to your leadership reinforces the importance of using the concepts discussed in this book, because they help you earn trust. And earning trust is equally important if the economy is strong, your organization is going like gangbusters, and your leadership decisions aren't magnified by the intensified scrutiny that comes when all hell breaks loose.

Leadership is about influencing others to do great things—regardless of the external circumstances—and all leadership happens within a context that's unique to leaders and their teams. The context might be the chaos of a start-up environment, the sometimes-stale stability of a large corporation, or the high-growth phase of a business that's scaling. And while the seas are sometimes calm, that context often includes disruptions—a major customer cancelling an order, a government issuing new restrictive guidelines, a natural disaster destroying a supplier's factory, a heated personality clash between two of your most valued employees, or a coronavirus halting almost all in-person interactions.

The context matters when it comes to the tactical decisions that leaders must make, which is why I wrote a chapter about the three distinct "climates" of leadership that exist today. Those climates—acceleration, access, and diversity—aren't going away because of a new crisis. If anything, their influence will only intensify. They shape the environment in which you lead and you need to be acutely aware of them, but they don't change the core of who you are or your philosophical approach to leadership. The values and principles of leadership remain constant, you just apply them differently in light of the realities you're facing and expecting to face. If you develop them and lean into them, they will help you navigate in any environment and set you up for success—for influencing others to do great things. That's the heart of the message in this book. That's the heart of *Transfluence.*

– Walt Rakowich, April 2020

PART I:
THE LEADERSHIP
ECOSYSTEM

YE CANNOT LIVE FOR YOURSELVES; A THOUSAND
FIBRES CONNECT YOU WITH YOUR FELLOW-MEN,
AND ALONG THOSE FIBRES, AS ALONG SYMPATHETIC
THREADS, RUN YOUR ACTIONS AS CAUSES, AND
RETURN TO YOU AS EFFECTS.
– HENRY MELVILL[1]

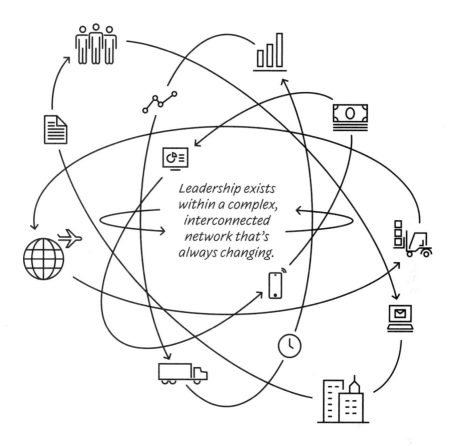

Leadership exists within a complex, interconnected network that's always changing.

L eadership exists within a complex, interconnected network—an ecosystem that's always changing, often in ways hard to predict. Figuring out how to navigate this landscape successfully is no easy matter, but something I call transformational influence is at the heart of finding the way forward. Understanding this ecosystem—its challenges and its opportunities—will prepare you for the next steps of growing into a leader who truly influences others to do great things. To begin this journey, we need a basic understanding of where we are, how we got there, and why we need to lead differently going forward. So that's where we'll start.

1.

AN EMERGING IDEA OF HOPE

ONLY A LIFE LIVED FOR OTHERS IS A LIFE WORTHWHILE.
– ALBERT EINSTEIN[2]

It's easy to grow discouraged by the state of affairs in our world, to see anger, bitterness, and divisiveness as the dominant themes of the day. Some pundits suggest our best years are behind us and that civilization, despite myriad technological advances, is rotting right before our eyes. Not me. I believe there is great hope for our future, and it lies in the hearts of emerging leaders.

That's not a generational term. Many emerging leaders are, in fact, young. They are the twenty-to-thirty-somethings who are just getting started in life and looking for ways to make a positive mark on the world. Some emerging leaders, however, are more seasoned. They've been working their way up the organizational ladder, and the windows of opportunity are opening for them to step through and lead in more formal ways. Others, still, are emerging from old styles of leadership. They've been "in charge," but the world around them is changing. Now they are exploring a better, more relevant version of themselves.

An emerging leader is simply anyone who is ready to take the next step in their leadership journey and embrace the challenges of the modern world. And I believe these leaders can have a transformative influence in their work, their families, and their communities. By overcoming the fears and pride that stunt their influence, by building transparency into their leadership, by developing a strong core of authentic values, and by passionately pursuing a meaningful purpose, they can seize the opportunities in front of them, embrace the challenges of society's complex climates, and make their organizations and communities greater than ever.

If you want to have that type of transformative influence, this book will help you do it.

Much of it is based on the lessons I learned during the crucible of leading the global real estate investment company Prologis from near bankruptcy back to a position as the undisputed leader in its industry. But that experience came after I had spent more than a decade helping Prologis grow into a giant in the industrial warehouse business.

At first, it seemed everything we touched turned to gold. When I started as a consultant to the company in 1993, Prologis was privately held with around fifty employees and about $50 million in assets. A year later, the company went public with an opening stock price of $11.50 per share. Over the next fourteen years, our assets grew to $36 billion, and the stock price climbed by more than 500 percent. This was after paying a hefty dividend each year to investors. During that stretch, I worked my way up the executive ladder, first as a senior vice president in charge of our operations in the mid-Atlantic states and then as chief financial officer. In 2007, by which time I was president and

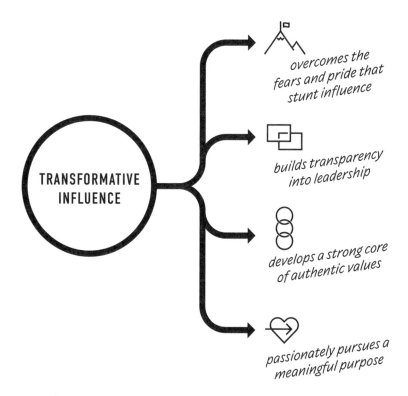

TRANSFORMATIVE INFLUENCE

overcomes the fears and pride that stunt influence

builds transparency into leadership

develops a strong core of authentic values

passionately pursues a meaningful purpose

chief operating officer, we had become a well-respected growth company in the S&P 500.

The good times, however, eventually began masking some near-fatal flaws in our leadership culture, which led me to step away from the company early in 2008. Then the Great Recession hit in full force, the company quickly fell on hard times, and the board asked me to return, this time as CEO. Four years later, the company was healthy again, and the time had come for me to hand the reins to new leadership. We orchestrated one of the biggest mergers in the history of the industry, and I stepped away from Prologis at the end of 2012.

With the help of my wife, a few close friends, and the Dallas-based Halftime organization, I began some soul-searching about how I could make a difference in the lives of others during the next phase of my life. Capturing what I'd learned about leadership emerged as one of the options.

Now, it's not unusual for leaders to write a "legacy" book to preserve the story of their journey or to write a book to promote some new venture like speaking or consulting. There's nothing wrong with those motives for writing a book, but those weren't my reasons. I was moved mainly by the challenges I saw emerging leaders facing and by the idea that some of what I'd learned along the way might help them rise to meet those challenges in some meaningful way.

There is practical value in the details of how we turned Prologis around, and that's a big part of my story. Those details, however, have a more powerful purpose as a backdrop to broader truths about leadership in our ever-changing culture. I didn't want to write about leadership unless I could confidently say I was adding something new to that much-discussed topic. After several false starts and a few changes in direction, I landed on a message I think is unique because it's based on timeless principles but applies them to the challenges and opportunities of modern leadership. So, while much of what you'll read in this book isn't new in theory, I think you will find that it is fresh and, in some ways, quite radical in how it must be practiced in the context of new realities.

To get to the final product, I had to go well beyond my experiences at Prologis. Some leaders define their leadership philosophy during a crisis. The really hard times cause them to take a deeper look at who they are and how they operate, and it can result in some fundamental changes in their leadership. I believe my trial-under-fire experience at Prologis exposed and refined my core ideas about leadership. In fact, had I not moved into that position with a strong foundation, I don't believe I would have survived the ordeal.

I trace my approach to leadership all the way back to my hardscrabble roots as the son of working-class parents in Pittsburgh. Neither of my parents had a college degree, but they taught me the value of things like working hard, treating people with respect, acting with integrity, and serving the greater good. Those concepts never go out of style, but living them isn't easy. It certainly wasn't always easy for me, and I believe it's even harder for leaders today.

The values my parents taught me were tested as I made my way through college at Penn State and began working in accounting and then real estate. I didn't always ace those tests, but I did my best to learn from them. Over the years, with the help of formal and informal training, I began to codify my ideas about my faith, my values, and my leadership, creating the deep footings that proved invaluable during my tumultuous tenure as CEO.

My leadership philosophy was and is pretty straightforward: leadership is about influencing others to do great things. It's an outward influence—one that's built on foundations of trust and that emphasizes service to others. I've spent the last few years evaluating that philosophy with a critical eye—studying what I've learned from my journey to make sure that approach is something more than just the linchpin to *my* story. I read books, articles, and blogs. I reviewed research. I talked to other leaders who have earned my respect. I wrote, reviewed, reflected, and edited. I sought opinions and advice. And as I refined my ideas into what you'll find in this book, I became convinced that they really will add significant value for emerging leaders around the world as they face unique and unprecedented leadership climates.

The result is a book about transformative influence—what it is and how to achieve it. I'll lay some groundwork by defining the climates that shape the modern leadership landscape, then build out an approach for leading in this complex environment. You'll learn how to chase your internal storms and deal with the fears and pride that come with leadership. You'll discover how to create a strong microclimate by looking outside the storms that surround you, embracing transparency, and developing a 3H-Core of humility, honesty, and heart. And you'll find how passion and meaningful purpose can make your leadership a force of nature.

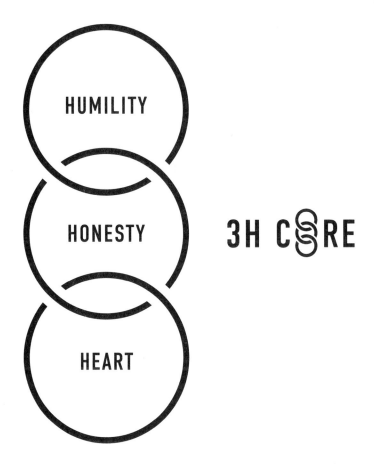

Along the way, I'll open up about many of the mistakes I've made and share stories from my trials and tribulations at Prologis. I'll offer advice from other leaders I interviewed and insights from my research. And I'll share what I call my "10 Fundamental Guideposts for Transfluence," a list of paradoxical truths that help us stay on the right path during our leadership journeys, even when that path is covered in blizzard-like conditions.

The guideposts were inspired by the work of Kent Keith. As a nineteen-year-old sophomore at Harvard, Keith began writing a booklet on leadership for high school students. It was first published in 1968, and Chapter 2 included his "paradoxical commandments" for leadership—ideas like, "People are illogical, unreasonable, and self-centered. Love them anyway." Keith wrote them as a challenge, he said, "to always do what is right and good and true, even if others don't appreciate it. You have to keep striving, no matter what, because if you don't, many of the things that need to be done in our world will never get done."[3]

You can (and should) read the original commandments at www.paradoxicalcommandments.com. But you also can find the full list, or a variety of spin-off versions, in books by all sorts of authors—Mother Teresa, Stephen R. Covey, Neil T. Anderson, John Maxwell. It's even in fictional works like Roger Stern's *Superman: The Never-Ending Battle*. So, with proper credit to Mr. Keith, I created my personal version as it relates to transfluence. They are sprinkled throughout the book. Like the originals, I hope you'll find them a challenge to do the right thing in life—no matter what.

Emerging leaders who are committed to doing the right things in life are the key to changing the trajectory of our world. The Brazilian author Paulo Coelho once said, "The world is changed by your example, not by your opinion."[4] So, if you are a pessimist in today's world, I hope this book will inspire you to lead with renewed hope. If you are an optimist, I hope it will fuel your desire to make the world a better place. And in either case, I hope it equips you to have a transformative influence on everyone around you.

CHAPTER RECAP

To make the most of this book, as with any experience in life, you'll need to internalize the message and adapt it to your personal experiences, beliefs, skills, goals, and dreams for the future. I'll end each chapter with a short recap to help you on your personal journey. Remember, leadership is about influencing others to do great things. It's an outward influence—one that's built on foundations of trust and that emphasizes service to others.

TRANSFLUENCE IN ACTION

+ Develop a mindset that inspires you to lead with hope and to have a transformative influence on everyone around you. Commit to doing the right things in life because that is the key to changing the trajectory of our world.

2.

→ # WELLSPRINGS OF LEADERSHIP

LOOK WITHIN. WITHIN IS THE FOUNTAIN OF THE GOOD, AND IT WILL EVER BUBBLE UP, IF THOU WILT EVER DIG.
– MARCUS AURELIUS[5]

History is full of stories about mythical springs with waters that heal the body and enrich the mind. You can find these tales in the cultures of Israel, India, across the Caribbean, and, of course, in Florida. But my favorite just might be one about the Macrobians of ancient Africa.

A Persian king, Cambyses II, conquered Egypt around 525 BC and decided he might as well take the rest of Africa while he was in the neighborhood. He didn't know much about this continent, however, so he sent representatives ahead of his army. The army didn't get very far—they were no match for the African geography, much less its people—but the scouts, mostly hired Africans, made it all the way to the western coast, the outer limits of the known world at the time. They returned with stories of a tribe so wealthy that it used shackles of gold on its prisoners. The men, they said, were extraordinarily tall and highly intelligent, not to mention darn good-looking. Not only that, but they lived to a ripe, old age of 120 years—on average.

These were the Macrobians.

Herodotus, the famous Greek historian who lived in the fifth century BC, heard about the tribe and preserved their story, including the scouts' explanation for the Macrobians' long lifespans and good fortunes. The Macrobians had discovered an extraordinary spring-fed pool. When they soaked in it, Herodotus was told, "they found their flesh all glossy and sleek, as if they had bathed in oil—and a scent came from the spring like that of violets."[6] Clearly, these mystical waters were the source of their success.

Oh, that we could take a dip into a pool and emerge healthy, wealthy, and wise!

I needed such waters when I became CEO of Prologis just as it hit rock bottom in the wake of the 2008 recession.

Prologis is a multinational commercial real estate enterprise. It owns and leases industrial warehouses, so I suspect that many readers of this book know very little, if anything, about it. It's not like Apple, Microsoft, Coke, or other more familiar consumer-focused companies. But this multibillion-dollar business-to-business enterprise touches the lives of millions of people, including you.

Indeed, Prologis is the largest owner of industrial facilities in the world. It owns and manages more than 4,600 facilities in nineteen countries across North America, South America, Asia, and Europe, serves more than 5,500 customers, employs 1,700 people, and has more than $118 billion in total assets under management.

That's close to 800 million square feet of warehouse space. Imagine 15,000 football fields with thirty feet of ceiling clearance, all stacked with goods. Companies like GE, Amazon, UPS, Walmart, and Procter & Gamble typically lease this space to store products before sending them to a retail outlet or directly to your home. Whatever you're wearing right now—your pants, your shoes, your socks, your shirt—more than likely made a stop in a warehouse. For that matter, most of the items around you, including the products you use on a daily basis (not to mention physical copies of this book), were housed in a warehouse during their journey through the supply chain.

I rose through the executive ranks at Prologis as it grew to become one of the best-performing companies in the S&P 500. In fact, as 2007 drew to a close, Prologis had provided stockholders with about a 19 percent compound annual return on their investment over close to a fourteen-year stretch since it went public. If you invested in the company's IPO, your return would have yielded more than ten times the original value over that period of time.

My career at Prologis, meanwhile, also had been storybook stuff. I thrived in the fast-paced and diverse world of international real estate investments and fed off the energy that comes with being involved in a high-growth organization filled with like-minded people. In 2004, however, our CEO retired. Little did

I know how dramatically the management team changes that followed would impact the direction of the company, not to mention my career.

Everything seemed great at first. I was promoted to president and chief operating officer, the leadership position second only to the new CEO, a highly intelligent growth-oriented leader who previously had run our international operations. Both of us joined the Prologis board, and we worked together reasonably well during those initial years.

By 2006 and 2007, however, there were chinks in the armor. More often than not, we found ourselves at odds, both on business decisions and on how to lead the company. We operated with a "growth-at-all-cost" mindset that was uncomfortable for me and many others on the leadership team. To me, the market felt frothy. We were expanding so rapidly that major decisions didn't get the due diligence and debate they deserved, and our balance sheet was looking more and more risky as we financed our growth with debt. Many others in the organization were sounding alarm bells as well, but it all seemed to get swept under the rug by our CEO, who saw such concerns as detrimental to the path of growth.

As time went on, we became isolated from one another, and our culture of shared trust devolved into one fueled by doubts. We found ourselves working in silos and failed miserably to compromise on a shared vision. I felt we needed to listen to each other and, in particular, listen to the concerns of our people. To the rest of us, it seemed like our CEO felt any opinion that didn't align with his was wrong.

Eventually, it became apparent that our CEO and I couldn't work effectively together. So, despite the company's success and my well-paying position, I decided to step down as president and chief operating officer in early 2008.

It was a good time to leave. At roughly $72 per share, our stock was trading near an all-time high, and the company was well-respected by our investors. I was only fifty at the time, but I had no immediate plans for my future. Technically, I was still on the Prologis payroll, so I spent a few months "phasing out"—cleaning up loose ends and helping identify my replacement. But by April I had pretty much checked out.

As spring rolled into summer, the company's stock had taken a sizable drop, falling by roughly 50 percent. The overall stock market also was down from the barrage of hits from the Great Recession but not nearly by as much. Were investors signaling a larger problem with the company? It was hard to tell. Actually, I didn't pay that much attention or give it much thought. I was personally more relaxed than I'd been in years. I had substantially increased my workout regimen and deepened my commitment to my family and my spiritual life.

When autumn rolled around, the company's stock price continued to nosedive just as I was looking into new opportunities. For the first time, I began to worry about the future of the company I'd left behind. The stock value had fallen more than 75 percent since the beginning of the year, investors were losing confidence, and members of the management team were sharing their concerns with me over internal issues that were getting worse by the day.

Things came to a head on November 8, 2008, when I got a call from the lead director of the Prologis board. The value of the company's stock had taken a ten-month tumble from $72 per share to nearly $5 per share. In the days that followed, it would bottom out at close to $2 per share. At that point, it was the third-worst performing stock in the S&P 500. Only General Growth Properties and AIG performed more poorly during that stretch. General Growth, you might recall, would file for bankruptcy protection, while the federal government would bail out AIG. And our situation wasn't much better. In what felt like the blink of an eye, Prologis had gone from king of the hill to the brink of bankruptcy. So, in an abrupt but anticipated move, the board decided to part ways with the CEO and, in that call, the lead director asked me to take his place. The management team was behind me, he said, and, in fact, was prepared to leave if I didn't take the job. He gave me twenty-four hours to make my decision.

Reluctantly, I agreed to return. At this point, the entire economy was in the grips of the recession. I knew it was going to take a Herculean effort, and I wasn't sure I was prepared to get it done. But I owed much of my professional success to this company, and I felt a deep sense of loyalty to its people. I was scared to death, but it wasn't about me. It was about the company. It was about saving jobs. I had to give it my best shot.

This was easily the most stressful period of my life. Not only were we in danger of going under, but our leadership team had grown dysfunctional. The fate of the company and everyone connected to it hung in the balance. And as we worked to rebuild a company that once was a darling of Wall Street, I realized we needed some radical changes.

When I searched my heart during those emotional, marathon workdays, I knew first and foremost we had to turn things around financially. But I also knew a turnaround wouldn't really mean that much or last that long without a complete restoration of trust. We needed to rebuild trust in each other and with everyone who was watching us—our board, our shareholders, our vendors, our customers. Everyone. I also knew that by restoring trust in our organization, we could restore perhaps an even more important opportunity—the ability to be influential in the lives of our people and in the people our organization touched.

My leadership philosophy was put to the test under some extreme circumstances over the next few years. I failed plenty during those trying times, but I came to appreciate the value of an approach to leadership that, as it turned out, was just what the company needed. And after nearly a decade of study and refinement, I'm convinced that this approach is even more relevant for the unique challenges leaders now face.

What I learned during the company's turnaround and in the years after was that the most powerful form of leadership is much like a Macrobian wellspring in that the experience results in a transformative influence. I call it *transfluence*. And unlike the legendary fountains of youth, transfluence is real and relevant for emerging leaders who represent the hope for our future.

What exactly is transfluence? Well, the dictionary defines *transfluent* as "flowing" or "running...through." The Macrobians could have talked about the "transfluent stream" that fed their mystical pools, for instance. Transfluence is very similar, because it flows from the heart of a leader. It's the essence of great leadership. Done well, it can change lives. Transfluence is leadership that is positively influential in a transformative way. And that's what we need from emerging leaders—today and in the future.

The principles that generate transformative influence were vital to the turnaround of Prologis, and, indeed, have been vital to leaders throughout time. I want to show you why these principles have never been more relevant and, more importantly, how they apply to the unique challenges of our

TRANSFLUENCE

=

LEADERSHIP THAT IS POSITIVELY INFLUENTIAL IN A TRANSFORMATIVE WAY.

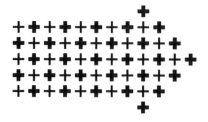

modern business climates. I believe leaders have a higher calling than ever, and living out that calling won't happen by clinging to the *status quo*. More like *mutare statum*—a state of change. To practice transfluence, we need to lean into those timeless values and principles, but with a fresh perspective on the new realities.

Leadership isn't easy, and it never has been. But the realities aren't the same as they were fifty years ago—or even ten or five years ago. In fact, the realities of our modern world are creating tensions and opportunities unlike anything we've ever seen—opportunities to do amazing things, but tensions that often prevent or deter us from reaching the very things we want and need. So, we need to innovate our leadership styles just as we innovate our products and services.

I'm a sports fan, so I'll summarize by using a football analogy. The realities of football are very different today than fifty years ago. The players are bigger, faster, and stronger. They have better equipment, nutrition programs, and training techniques. And the game has moved from ground-and-pound to throw-and-go. But the fundamentals of the game—things like blocking, tackling, mental focus, limiting turnovers—are no less important. They just have to be understood and applied based on new realities. So, to create transformative influence as leaders, we have to thoroughly understand some timeless values and, just as importantly, learn how they can best serve us in the climates that are reshaping our world.

It would be convenient if we could soak in the healing Macrobian waters and emerge transformed and equipped with all the insights we need to lead in the future. Instead, we have to do some hard work, much of it self-reflective. Author Jon Gordon refers to this as the Law of the Skyscraper, because great leaders, like great skyscrapers, are built first by digging deep into the ground to create a foundation of stability.

"It's not always easy to unearth the stuff below (the fears we have, the wounds we carry and the things that hold us back)," Gordon points out, "but once we uncover them, we can reach the core of our foundation and begin the building process to reach greater heights."[7]

Leaders who are willing to take this journey of self-discovery will find themselves uniquely fortified for the opportunities and challenges of the future. But first, they need to understand the changing climates that are shaping that future.

CHAPTER RECAP

Sometimes your toughest challenges create opportunities for dipping into your wellsprings of leadership. Real leadership starts by building trust. Without trust, you have no platform from which to build. Great leaders build trust so that they can have transformative influence on the people they lead. I call it transfluence. Transfluent leaders have a fresh perspective on the new realities of the leadership climates in which we live, but they are not afraid to lean into timeless values and principles to effectively deal with those realities.

TRANSFLUENCE IN ACTION

+ Begin by evaluating your environment and the way in which you lead. Is it an environment of trust? Building a foundation of timeless values and principles will help you succeed in creating the environment you desire.

GUIDEPOST NO. 1

HARSH CLIMATES BRING
TOUGH CHALLENGES.

EMBRACE EVERY ONE OF THEM.

3.

CLIMATES OF CHANGE

NATURE IS SO POWERFUL, SO STRONG. CAPTURING ITS ESSENCE IS NOT EASY – YOUR WORK BECOMES A DANCE WITH LIGHT AND THE WEATHER. IT TAKES YOU TO A PLACE WITHIN YOURSELF.
– ANNIE LEIBOVITZ[8]

Prologis operates globally, so working for the company took me around the world. And my wife and I have had some fantastic personal vacations over the years. For work or pleasure, and often both, I've been fortunate to visit parts of Africa, Asia, Europe, and North, Central, and South America. We've visited islands, mountain tops, lakes, and rivers, and we've gazed upon some of the most beautiful spots on Earth. But I'm hard pressed to describe a more remarkable and memorable trip than the one Sue and I took at the start of 2018.

The three-week cruise began in Buenos Aires, Argentina, and took us down to Antarctica for six days. Then we sailed through the Drake Passage and up the Pacific coastline, ending in San Antonio, Chile, just west of Santiago. It was an adventure of a lifetime to us, but it didn't start out that way. In fact, we went into it with extremely modest expectations. When we booked the trip, I saw it as a chance to relax and detach—to enjoy one-on-one time with Sue, see some new sites, and catch up on my reading. Sue thought the trip would be interesting, but she wondered if we'd both quickly become bored after a few days of standing on the deck of a cruise ship dressed in heavy coats and watching ice float by.

Instead, we were mesmerized by the natural beauty of this part of the planet. The temperatures were chilly during the southernmost parts of the journey, but it was never unbearable, and, frankly, it was warmer than we expected. The opportunity to learn so much, both from the experts aboard the ship and from the experiences, kept our attention like no other trip we'd ever made. I took hundreds of photos, listened to lectures, and took every opportunity to watch seals, whales, seabirds, and penguins. Even the icebergs were interesting. I read almost nothing that didn't have to do with the habitats and environments we were exploring. And I spent hours reflecting on things like life, leadership, God, creation, the wonders of nature, and my place in this vast universe. As the cruise neared its end, Sue mentioned that she felt she could stay for weeks more without getting bored, and I fully agreed.

One of the things I took on the trip was an early draft of this book, which I figured I would read a few times and take notes about the revisions and edits I wanted to make. As you might expect, I never touched the manuscript. But the trip contributed to my thinking in many ways, and not the least of which was by affirming my view of the opportunities and the challenges that come with the climates around us.

The climates in and around Antarctica are dynamic. The cold winds, ice, changing ocean currents, and rising sea levels are among the many factors that constantly shape and reshape the environment. Many of the lectures we heard discussed how the continent is changing and what that means for all of us. It reminded me that we all, humans and other living creatures, have to seize opportunities and overcome challenges as we deal with the climates we're in.

Climates are an unavoidable component of every environment. They have basic characteristics, but they don't stay exactly the same from day to day; they influence what we do and how we do it; and they can be influenced over time but not fully controlled. They attract all sorts of animals that thrive in certain conditions, some friendly and some not. And they bring storms, sunshine, rainbows, and clouds—sometimes all on the same day.

As the great pundit Anonymous put it, "Climate is what we expect, weather is what we get."[9]

Most of us live in a climate defined by historical weather trends that give us some idea of what to expect from season to season. The environment for leadership, however, is more complex, because it exists at the convergence of three dynamic climates: access, diversity, and acceleration. Each is independently distinguishable, but all three are present at the same time. It's like living in some

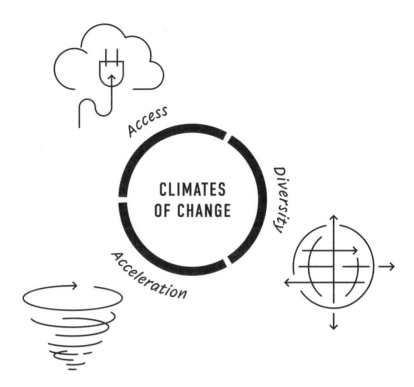

mystical land where polar, tropical, and desert climates all co-exist. Just figuring out how to dress is a challenge.

That these climates exist and impact the world in which we live and lead isn't up for debate. I experienced them firsthand as a leader at Prologis. Their influence has only grown stronger in recent years, and they will continue to dominate the workforce environment for the foreseeable future. How they impact and shape our world is in some ways obvious but in many other ways quite hard to figure. I can say with confidence, however, that these climates, either on their own or in aggregate, are producing significant opportunities and tensions that will challenge leaders for generations.

This book isn't about the climates per se, but it is all about what it takes to lead effectively within those climates. Our challenge is to navigate in this environment with precision and purpose, using the enduring principles of transfluence to bridge the gaps between the fast-paced, diverse world and the basic needs of people around us. To do that successfully, we need to understand these climates and then apply timeless values in ways that augment their realities. So, let's first take a deeper look at each.

THE CLIMATE OF ACCESS:
THE REALITIES CREATED BY OUR UNPRECEDENTED ACCESS
TO INFORMATION AND PEOPLE.

Let's face it: We live and work in a world of glass houses. Everything we do stands bare in the windows of the digital age for anyone to see. Our words. Our strategies. Our actions. Our policies. Our products and services. The cultures we create. All of it.

We live in a hyper-connected, global culture that's tethered by technology. In January 2019, 28 percent of Americans said they were online "almost constantly" and another 45 percent said they were online "several times a day." The percentages were even higher among younger Americans, but they were on the rise in every age category.[10] Phones, tablets, watches—pretty much anything—now can connect the world's 4.4 billion active internet users to the web. More than 2 billion of those are using social media. By 2022, the number of internet users is expected to reach 6 billion, and a full 90 percent of the projected world population age six and older— some 7.5 billion people—will be using the internet by 2030.[11]

And not only is everything more visible, there's more to see. Åse Dragland of the European-based research company SINTEF pointed out in 2013 that 90 percent of the world's data had been created in the previous two years.[12] Many researchers say that's been true for more than thirty years, and the trend continues with 2.5 quintillion bytes of data created each day.[13] That's tons of tweets, YouTube views, texts, Instagram posts, Google searches, and spam e-mails (among so, so many other things).

This climate of access generates amazing opportunities. Access to big data and super-charged analytics, for instance, provides a competitive advantage for organizations willing and able to use it. Teams, meanwhile, can collaborate in exciting new ways, using cloud-based software and advanced applications to connect our work even when we're physically separated. And we can crowdsource everything from vacation policies to the organization's giving strategy, using shared access for shared decision-making that strengthens a shared sense of purpose.

Greater access also drives leaders and organizations to higher and higher levels of accountability. Websites focus on exposing corruption, leaking sensitive documents, or providing opportunities for employees to anonymously rate and discuss their employers. Access to information provides insights into the details of a leader's world—the good and the bad. Untrustworthy leaders are more quickly exposed, and employees can make more informed decisions about where they prefer to work.

But there are a number of challenging implications to all of this access.

One, greater access can fuel collaboration, but, paradoxically, it often causes us to make decisions in a vacuum. We have access to so much information that we can dismiss input from others. We trust Google but risk missing the firsthand knowledge and experiences of the people around us.

Perhaps this explains why a 2018 survey of more than 20,000 adults found that 46 percent "sometimes or always" feel alone, 27 percent "rarely or never feel as though there are people who really understand them," and 43 percent "sometimes or always feel that their relationships are not meaningful."[14]

Author Enuma Okoro pointed out that, "the false sense of intimacy created in the virtual world fails to satisfy people's real needs for knowing others and being known by others ... After all, being lonely is not necessarily about a-lone-ness, but about a lack of intimate, meaningful connection."[15]

Two, embedded in the glut of information is the overabundance of false narratives that create an uncertainty about who or what to believe.

ACCESS / BY THE NUMBERS

90%
*of the world (age 6+)
will be using the
internet by 2030*

2.5
*quintillion bytes
of data are
created each day*

46%
*of adults "sometimes
or always" feel alone*

Plenty was written about attempts by Russians to influence the 2016 US elections, but it's not just governments, politicians, and marketers who are trying to control what we read and see on the internet. Most folks don't go to the extreme measures used to disrupt the elections, but many people, even ordinary users, make some attempt to control their message on the internet with photoshopped pictures, carefully crafted narratives, and strategic button-pushing.

One social commentator pointed out that perhaps the "biggest obstacle to truth in today's post-truth world isn't falsehood. It's confusion."[16] Whether it's outright fabrications, twisting the truth, or manipulating the context, it all contributes to a lack of trust in others and what they have to say or contribute.

Three, our conversations are more digital and less face-to-face or voice-to-voice.

Admit it: You've seen at least one meme with a photo of teenagers standing together, each staring at their smartphones, and another photo, this one from twenty or so years ago, of teens laughing and skipping rocks at a creek. Not only did you sigh, but you shared it—or at least thought about sharing it. But it's not just teens who are tethered to technology. We all can communicate with a click or a swipe, which is often efficient and at times effective. But it tends to weaken our conversational and social skills as they atrophy from lack of exercise.

Regardless of our age, it's often convenient and easy to hide behind our devices rather than engaging others, especially if that engagement might involve a difficult topic.

And, four, there's an unprecedented freedom and pressure to share everything about ourselves.

We have a natural and instinctive need for approval—to feel loved and to feel relevant. We have grown accustomed to more instant feedback and gratification. And we feel drawn to show people who we are and what our best looks like. The digital world allows us to play out our performances with scale and on bigger stages. All of this pushes us to focus on ourselves and our image—even when we might be championing a cause or advocating for others. The emphasis on self-image can create challenges for admitting and addressing our failures and weaknesses. And it creates tensions with the fundamental leadership qualities that all leaders should cultivate—like seeing life itself as a gift or sacrificing to serve the needs of others.

THE CLIMATE OF DIVERSITY:
THE REALITIES CREATED BY THE WORLD'S INCREDIBLE DIVERSITY—
NOT JUST IN PEOPLE, BUT IN THE WAYS WE COLLABORATE AND IN
THE WAYS WE LIVE AND WORK.

The size of the planet hasn't changed dramatically over the course of history, but we're no longer relegated to interacting primarily with nearby neighbors who look like us and think like us. Instead, a high percentage of people in the world regularly interact with other people who are significantly different from themselves.

In the mid-1990s, for instance, 80 percent of the content on the web was in English. Now, ten languages make up 82 percent of the content.[17] One-third of the residents in the US are now classified as minorities. And more than 8 million businesses in America are minority-owned, according to the Minority Business Development Agency.[18]

Those numbers speak to the traditional view of diversity, which is the reality that we work daily with people of different races, genders, nationalities, and cultures. Even within that, there are often-ignored components such as educational diversity, social class diversity, experiential diversity, generational diversity, personality diversity, and "ability" diversity (roughly 15 percent of the global population—more than a billion people—live with some type of physical, mental, or communicative disability[19]).

Much of the world, especially the more economically developed nations, has seen a steady progression in the evolution of diversity in its traditional sense. We've gone from advocating for people to advocating for a voice, then a vote, then a place at the table, and now positions of influence. There's still room for improvement, but women and minorities have a greater voice in business than ever. And Generation Z already makes up more than 32 percent of the global population, so its collective voice is becoming more and more relevant. Bloomberg research estimates the Gen Z population was at 61 million in the US in 2019, and its spending power was at more than $143 billion—even though most of them were still in school.[20]

Having a voice is one thing, but groups also want a vote—they want a say in what's happening. That includes voting in elections, but it also includes sharing opinions and rallying with like-minded friends and colleagues. At work, diverse groups are seeking a place at the table. They want to help make decisions, and, while progress has been slow on this front[21], some boards and leadership teams are recognizing the value of a wide range of backgrounds and perspectives. As they find a place at the table, they are positioned to bring influence as leaders. They are finding they have the power to create change.

As a board member for some major public companies, I can personally attest to the reality that there's a push by diverse groups of stakeholders to define how organizations are governed. Employees want their identity labels to be recognized, and shareholders want to make sure certain groups are represented.

Diversity, however, is a much larger concept than many leaders realize. In addition to the traditional diversity of people, there's geographic diversity. Companies work on a more global level. In fact, a 2013 report by McKinsey Global Institute predicts that nearly half of the world's biggest companies will be based in emerging markets by 2025. Even smaller companies—all the way down to the mom-and-pop retailer or the freelancer—are likely to have global suppliers, customers, and/or clients.

The workforce, enabled by greater access, also is more distributed. People work out of homes, airplanes, coffee shops, subway stations, and the like. They

DIVERSITY / BY THE NUMBERS

10

languages make up 82 percent of the content on the web

1/2

of the world's biggest companies will be based in emerging markets by 2025

8+

million businesses in America are minority-owned

work on vacations, on weekends, and at all times during the day. More than 57 million Americans worked as freelancers in 2019, and 60 percent of them were doing so by choice rather than necessity.[22] Mercer's Global Talent Trends 2019, meanwhile, reported that 82 percent of employees say they are willing to consider freelance work. "This figure is even higher in Mexico (94%), China (93%), Hong Kong (92%), and the Middle East (92 %)," the report said.[23]

And then there's the diversity of choice. Go to Walmart.com, for instance, and search for jelly. I did that one day and found thirty-four pages of results—more than 1,300 options. Whether we're picking a jelly or a job, we have an overwhelming array of options.

All of this diversity presents amazing opportunities for collaboration and cross-pollination of ideas. But that doesn't mean leading in this climate is easy. There are tensions that leaders must acknowledge and address. Among them:

+ Diversity can create expectations that are difficult to manage. First, it increases the expectation of customization—not just of products and services to meet a diverse market but also of job descriptions, employee benefits, work schedules, and work spaces. Second, it increases the expectation that every opinion on every issue is not only valid but worth adopting. These expectations often lead to positive changes, but it is not always possible, or healthy, to give everyone or every group everything on their wish list.

+ While diversity can draw people together, it also can draw them into cliques or into isolationism, both of which can breed distrust. Sometimes it's uncomfortable to communicate with people who are different. The remedy often is silence—which, of course, is an all-too-convenient option for avoiding conflict.

+ The global economy provides opportunities to buy, sell, partner in, and influence more and more markets, but it requires a deeper appreciation of those cultures. The fact that it's easier than ever to work away from a centralized team provides freedom, but it requires accountability and different ways of building trust among coworkers who might seldom spend time face-to-face.

✦ The diversity of choice can be both liberating and paralyzing. Endless opportunities lose their value when leaders either pick no option because they can't stop debating their merits or pick too many options because they want to do it all. They either end up with no jelly for their toast or a pantry full of flavors they'll never get around to tasting.

THE CLIMATE OF ACCELERATION:
THE REALITIES CREATED BY THE LIGHTNING-FAST SPEED OF CHANGE.

Most leaders will tell you that the world is moving faster than ever—that the pace of work and the pace of change is creating unpredictability like never before and that tomorrow things will only move faster. There's little comfort in the fact that the world—good, old planet Earth—is actually moving slower. Atomic clocks indicate our days are about 1.7 milliseconds longer than a century ago.

Great! That's nearly two extra milliseconds to squeeze in more of... something!

One of the consistent markers of the human race is our insatiable drive for progress. And yet, progress requires change, and change is uncomfortable. With every decade, change comes faster and faster. We welcome the advantages and conveniences that change can bring. If we stumble upon an unfamiliar word, we can ask our phone—or some other voice-activated device that's connected to the Internet of Things—and have an answer within seconds. Artificial intelligence is advancing so quickly that one of your devices might be reading—and having emotional responses to—this book that it will share with you in your book club. Much of the developed world has speed-climbed Maslow's hierarchy of needs.[24] We no longer spend days traveling a few hundred miles or wait weeks for a letter so we can learn the "latest" news from friends and loved ones who don't live nearby. Everything we need, and most of what we want, is available and convenient. With the basics taken care of, we can devote our energy to esteem and self-actualization.

But many of the world's advancements have us wigged out. Artificial intelligence and automation, for instance, breed fears among those who see them as a threat to their personal livelihoods. Consider the typical account representative at a large company who has traditionally taken and managed client orders over the phone. Now those clients can place and manage their orders online and track them on their phone or tablet. Rather than engaging in the changing world and finding a better place in it, those account reps, and workers in similar situations, face a temptation to resist—to isolate themselves, withhold information and ideas, or disrupt progress in hopes of building job security.

Even those who are willing and able to adapt to the changing times fear that they might lose their jobs in favor of younger, more tech-savvy workers with less experience but smaller salaries. And there might just be some merit to those fears. IBM CEO Ginni Rometty told attendees at the IBM Think 2018 conference that business and technology are converging in ways that happen about once every twenty-five years and that, "it has the potential to change everything."[25] That change will cost some workers their jobs, she admits, but it also creates the need for what she calls, "new collar" workers who have the "ability to work with technology in everything you do."[26]

The blazing speed of the modern world keeps us well-informed, which can lead to more timely decisions and, especially for nimble organizations, pivots that create tremendous competitive advantages. At the same time, the accelerated pace creates pressure to act without context, which often results in flawed decisions.

While instantly accessing boatloads of information can help us respond quickly to challenges, its pounding presence can create a distraction that

ACCELERATION / BY THE NUMBERS

6x

faster – the rate at which 1,500 people on social media are more likely to hear a falsehood than a truth

375

million workers worldwide may have to switch occupations by 2030 because of advances in digitization and AI

220

seconds – the time it takes Google's quantum computer to solve a complex problem that the most advanced classical computer needs 10,000 years to solve diverts our focus toward the trivial and away from people, rest, or purpose. We have less time for others, or even for ourselves, while pouring our attention into the information that arrives non-stop at our fingertips.

The pressure to work non-stop can erode work-life balance and creates a heightened pressure to perform or risk getting left behind, especially in sectors like tech and finance. In some cases, people are working themselves to death. The Japanese actually have a word that describes this: karoshi, which literally means "overworked death." There were 189 deaths in Japan in 2015 that were attributed to *karoshi*, ninety-three from suicides and the rest from heart attacks, strokes, and other illnesses directly related to overwork.[27]

Despite the ever-so-gradual slowing of the earth's rotation, leaders are squeezed for time when it comes to adopting to the new environments that define how work gets done. All of this makes disciplines like rest, reflection, and contemplation difficult to embrace, even though, paradoxically, they are central to wise decision-making and healthy leadership.

Psychologist Stephanie Brown, author of *Speed: Facing Our Addiction to Fast and Faster and Overcoming Our Fear of Slowing Down*, says the culture of instant gratification and no limits actually creates an addictive high.

"What are the costs of speed addiction?" Brown asked. "We live under a weight of demands, real and imagined, that is debilitating. We see an alarming increase in stress-related disorders of all kinds for all ages, beginning with elementary school-age children who are struggling with obesity, depression, anxiety, attention disorders and all kinds of learning disabilities, a list of problems for all ages."[28]

Acceleration creates a vicious cycle, she said, because it promotes overstimulation and overscheduling that create stress, which affects our health, moods, and behaviors, and so we try to work faster and harder (and we likely overmedicate), all in an effort to keep up with expectations, real or perceived.

CONFLICT IN THE CLIMATES

Together, these three climates create realities (positive, negative, and in between) that impact how everyone thinks, feels, and behaves. On one hand, they allow us greater access to a variety of things at lightning speed. They result in progress that was unimaginable in years past. More and better information rapidly acquired from unique perspectives enables us to make highly informed decisions. That's good. On the other hand, these climates can cause us to feel intimidated, overwhelmed, and underappreciated. They can make us more skeptical and less open-minded. And they can leave us too busy to keep up and too distracted to focus.

In short, while these climates often produce healthy desires, legitimate needs, and amazing opportunities for progress, they simultaneously form storms that can block us from fulfilling those desires, meeting those needs, and experiencing that growth. And that creates a very challenging environment for leaders.

If you ask leaders what they would like to see in their workforces, for instance, they will tell you that this rapidly changing and more diverse world is creating the need for more collaboration, more communication, more interaction, and more openness. When PwC interviewed more than a thousand CEOs, a wide majority mentioned that they were looking for skills that machines can't perform such as leadership and emotional intelligence. And if you ask most emerging leaders, they will tell you they want more mentorship, more personal growth, and more purpose in their jobs.

Given all of the challenges associated with greater access, growing diversity, and the pace of acceleration, the world craves leaders who demonstrate a high degree of empathy, transparency, and authenticity. Leaders who look outward to others and not inward to themselves. Leaders who can hold diverse groups accountable and yet be sensitive to their changing needs. Leaders who can demonstrate quick thinking and decisive action with informative openness during the process. And leaders who demand excellence at high speeds but also bring a sense of balance and purpose to their lives and the lives of those around them.

That's all easier said than done, of course, but transfluence isn't impossible, and it's certainly worth the effort. It begins with a simple, timeless premise: Leadership is not about you; it's about the influence you have on those you touch. From that starting point, we can follow a prescriptive path of self-discovery that unpacks and applies the universal truths and innovative best practices. These values weren't born in the digital age, but they provide the foundation for managing access, diversity, and acceleration in ways that build trust and serve the greater good. Thus, they shape our quest for transformative influence within the complex climates of our modern world.

CHAPTER RECAP

Our modern leadership environment exists at the convergence of three distinct and dynamic climates: the climates of access, diversity, and acceleration. Greater access, while enhancing productivity, can lead to less collaboration, false narratives, and less personal interaction. Greater diversity, while widening our spectrum, can be more difficult to manage, can lead to isolationism, and can be less personal given a more distributed workforce. Greater acceleration, while enabling competitive advantages, can also create enormous pressures, distractions, and work-life imbalances. On their own or in the aggregate, those climates are producing significant opportunities and tensions that will challenge leaders for generations.

TRANSFLUENCE IN ACTION

+ Don't let the harsh storms of our modern climates block you from leading in a transfluent way. Develop a fundamental understanding of these climates while keeping this simple, timeless premise in mind: Leadership is not about you; it's about the influence you have on others. Your ability to grasp this in all you do will enhance your leadership success, regardless of the climates surrounding you.

PART II: CHASING YOUR STORMS

THE DEVIL WHISPERS, 'YOU CANNOT WITHSTAND THE
STORM.' THE WARRIOR REPLIES, 'I AM THE STORM.'
– UNKNOWN

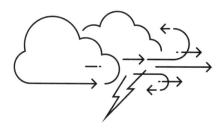

TRANSFLUENT LEADERS NEED COURAGE TO CONFRONT THE STORMS THEY FACE.

Leadership requires courage because it takes us to uncomfortable places. Like the storm chasers who rush toward a tornado, transfluent leaders need courage to confront the storms they face. The most significant storms, however, aren't external. Instead, they are the storms that live within. So, before we talk about the timeless values of transfluence, we need to understand the ageless leadership challenges of fears and pride—and why access, diversity, and acceleration make them even more daunting to leaders today than ever. Because before we can be a transformative influence, we must chase these internal storms and the personal demons that create them.

GUIDEPOST NO. 2

STORMS RAGE FROM DEEP WITHIN US AND CONFRONTING THEM IS PAINFUL.

ENDURE THE PAIN.

4.

 # DAZED BUT UNCONFUSED

YOU MAY NOT CONTROL ALL THE EVENTS THAT HAPPEN TO YOU, BUT YOU CAN DECIDE NOT TO BE REDUCED BY THEM.
– MAYA ANGELOU[29]

I was returning to one of the most intense meetings of my life, and there was no hiding the knot on my head. Clearly, I had some explaining to do.

It was early December 2008, just a few weeks after my return to Prologis. The situation I had inherited had gone from bad to awful. And the forecast called for it to get worse.

A combination of factors was at play. The Great Recession, which the International Monetary Fund labeled the worst global recession since World War II[30], had made things financially difficult for all businesses. But the severe economic downturn was just part of the story. We also had made some poor business decisions in the months and years leading up to the recession, many of them the result of a dysfunctional leadership culture. Internal missteps and external forces had sent the company's stock spiraling downward. The financial walls were closing in like the jaws of a starving shark, and the climates we discussed in the previous chapter were merging in ways that created a mega storm like nothing I had seen before or since.

I knew we had problems, but I had vastly underestimated most of them. The realities began hitting me on my first day back, which I recall like it was yesterday. I picked up *The Wall Street Journal*, as I usually did each morning, and saw our situation summed up in a headline: "Warehouse Owner Prologis Hits a Wall." One senior analyst accurately pointed out that Prologis had fallen because it was "overleveraged and counting on good economic times."[31] Other analysts openly predicted bankruptcy.

Talk about access and acceleration! Events were happening so fast that I couldn't follow them. Frankly, I felt like I was shooting down Class VI rapids in a kayak without a paddle, dodging rocks that were coming my way at the speed of light. It seemed like millions of people were looking at everything we did through a microscopic lens. We were living in our own glass house, and I wondered if it was about to shatter.

I must have had more than a thousand "urgent" calls, emails, and texts that first day from equity and bond investors, bankers, sell side analysts, rating agencies, news publications, and local politicians, all wanting answers to a variety of questions. They weren't asking for answers; they were demanding answers. Online chats were rampant with discussion about our future and my leadership. I found out all sorts of things about what people thought of me, some good and some bad. It amazed me what people felt empowered to say when they could hide behind the veil of the internet. I also received congratulatory calls and emails from friends, employees, and our board, but I had no time to return them. Besides, I wasn't sure I felt like I had earned something that rose to the level of "congratulations."

The top priority was simple: survive. We had to make sweeping changes, and we had to make them quickly. The decisions we made—or failed to make— would impact thousands of investors, as well as the lives of our employees around the world. There was no time to waste and very little margin for error.

As you might imagine, our leadership team began working late into the nights looking for solutions. On one such night, our treasurer, chief financial officer, and seven or eight other financial analysts were with me in the doom-and-gloom conference room discussing some harsh realities. Our earnings were projected to plummet, and we were faced with drastically writing down the value of our real estate holdings. We had more than $10 billion in outstanding debt coming due in the next eighteen months with little collateral to refinance it. We were close to blowing certain covenants on many of our bonds, and our creditors were getting more anxious by the day. Somewhere after midnight, the discussion turned to Chapter 11 bankruptcy protection— not *if we would file*, but *when we would file*.

"How much time do we have?" I asked.

"Two, maybe three months," I was told.

I felt the energy drain from my face, and I suspect I turned white as a ghost. I rubbed my temples and searched for answers as the group looked to me for direction.

I was no stranger to leadership. I had been in charge of projects and teams. I had been responsible for large portions of the business. I had made tough decisions and dealt with challenging issues. But this was different. I was experiencing the pressures of leadership in a very new and uncomfortable way. Now I was the CEO—Chief Everything Officer. Now the biggest decisions were in my hands. No one out-ranked me. No one would overrule me. But no one would rescue me if I was uncertain about what to do. In fact, when others were uncertain about what we should do, they now turned to me—and no one else.

I was physically, intellectually, and emotionally exhausted. Never had I felt so unsure about things, so unsteady in my course, so ill-equipped to lead. I thought about all the people I knew and cared for who worked for Prologis. I thought about the people in the room who needed my leadership. I thought about my family. With the crisis swirling around us, I was feeling the weight of my new title and the weight of the company's future on my shoulders. It might as well have been the weight of the world.

As the pressure and anxiety mounted in my mind, I bought myself the one thing I needed most—time.

"I need a few minutes," I told the group, and I left the conference room to get a drink of water and clear my head.

The hallway on the fifth floor of our corporate headquarters in Denver seemed more narrow than usual. As I walked toward my office, I became dizzy, and the floor seemed unsteady beneath my feet. It quickly became apparent that I was about to faint, so I stepped into the first office I came to in search of a chair. My legs began to melt like butter on a hot roll. And in the darkness of that empty office, I passed out cold.

When I awoke about ten minutes later, I wasn't sure where I was or how I'd gotten there. I took several slow, deep breaths and tried to gather my wits and my bearings. My head throbbed from a lump above my brow. I looked down to see blood forming into a dark red pool on the green carpet. My fall had taken me headfirst into the corner of a desk, leaving a nasty gash above my eye to go with the knot on my head.

I sat up on the floor and pressed my palm against the cut to slow the bleeding. My head still throbbed, but my mind became crystal clear about a hard truth: everyone in the conference room was waiting for me to return, and I still didn't have any answers.

This isn't an easy admission for any leader, especially one at the top of the org chart. We're in charge because we are supposed to be the "expert." In times of turmoil, all eyes fall on the leader. Everyone is looking to the leader to bring the team out of the wilderness. The leader must respond with confidence, passion, purpose, and solutions. I had the passion, I knew our purpose, and I thought we would somehow figure things out. But I was woefully short on solutions.

When I returned to the conference room, it easily had been twenty minutes since I had asked for the break. As I walked in, I was still thinking through what I would say and how I would say it. I was gripped by fear but too proud to admit my insecurities. I tried to restart the meeting as if nothing had happened, but I felt the collective gaze of the group as it locked onto my battered face. I looked back blankly until someone broke the awkward silence.

"What the hell happened to your head?" the voice said.

I'm in prison, I thought. *There's no way out.*

I couldn't hide, and denial no longer was an option.

Still unsteady on my feet, still unsure of exactly what to say or do, I briefly told them how I'd passed out and hit my head. Then I did something every leader I know struggles to do: I let go. I became vulnerable. I took a deep breath and spoke directly from my heart.

"Look, I don't know what to say," I told them. "I simply don't know what to do. Frankly, I don't have the answers. I really don't. I need your help."

Everybody looked at me, and for a moment there was complete silence as if no one knew what to say. Then something amazing happened, something that lifted my confidence in ways I never could have imagined. There was a tremendous outpouring of support. Here's the gist of what they said: "We're with you, Walt. Don't worry about it. We'll figure it out."

In that moment, I had a deeper appreciation than ever for the incredible power of vulnerability. I had shown vulnerability as a leader throughout my career but never under such extreme circumstances. And, frankly, it somehow seemed like the wrong thing to do. I was supposed to be the rock, and a rock is

VULNERABILITY ISN'T A TOOL YOU ABANDON AS YOU CLIMB THE CORPORATE LADDER BECAUSE IT FORCES YOU TO TRUST OTHERS AND EARNS YOU TRUST IN RETURN.

solid—not vulnerable. But I realized vulnerability isn't a tool you abandon as you climb the corporate ladder—it's a tool you can't lead effectively without. It's a tool that forces you to trust others, and it's a tool that earns you trust in return.

When you recognize your weaknesses, and you tell people that you don't have it all together, they will do just about anything to help you. Why? Because they see themselves in you. They know you aren't infallible. They know you have the same problems that they do. They know you are experiencing the same fears that they are facing. When you put aside your pride and admit your fears, you defeat them. And people respond to it in a positive way. I didn't recognize what a strong tool sharing vulnerability was until that night. There's real power in it.

It was through this experience that I gained a deeper understanding and perspective of the roles fear and pride play in the life of a leader. Chasing these two storms is essential for leaders who want to have transformative influence. I became a different person that night in the eyes of the people in that room. And stories like that get out very quickly. They become folklore, and people ask you about it. I was happy to talk about it, which I believe strengthened the trust and commitment that came from showing vulnerability.

By the way, we did figure it out. Not that night, of course. But over many hours, days, weeks, and months, and with the help of many committed people, we went from "awful" to somewhat better, to much better, until eventually we returned to great—and not just great financially but great as an organization.

The transformation, however, began when we recognized the real source of our problems: us.

Over a three-to-four-year period prior to the recession, our financial success had masked a management team that didn't listen to each other, that didn't trust each other, and that wasn't earning the support of its employees. As a result, we were in a weakened position to withstand the economic storms that battered us and nearly led to our downfall. I realized the fears and pride of the previous administration were the root of our problems, and the new management team had to operate in a different way. We no longer could run from that reality. We had to chase our storms so we could regain our influence in the changing climates of our times.

It's never been more important for leaders to chase our storms, and that starts by understanding our personal fears and our pride. Most bad decisions are fueled by fear and pride, and they are exacerbated by the climates in which we live. Climates where people shoot first and ask questions later. Climates where you and your glass house are on display for everyone to see. Climates where fear and pride battle within the heart of every leader, destroying trust at every opportunity. But they don't have to win. Chase them down. Confront them. And then you'll experience the inner transformative influence that allows you to build trust and influence others to do great things.

CHAPTER RECAP

Crucible moments happen to every leader. It's how you handle them that matters. Unfortunately, our internal storms at times prevent us from leading effectively. Sometimes it helps to let go and be vulnerable. But vulnerability is tough for prideful, insecure leaders. It's not a trait you'll read about in most leadership books. But it's authentic and, as such, it is appreciated by those you influence. It positions a leader to rely on others, and thus is one of the most powerful ways you can act in creating trust.

TRANSFLUENCE IN ACTION

+ Don't let the internal storms within you prevent or disrupt authentic leadership. These storms are almost always caused by fear or pride. A critical step in your leadership journey is to admit those storms exist so you can chase them and deal with them effectively.

GUIDEPOST NO. 3

FEAR AND PRIDE CAN DRIVE
THE DECISIONS OF LEADERS.

DON'T GIVE THEM CONTROL.

5.

THE FACES OF FEAR

NO PASSION SO EFFECTUALLY ROBS THE MIND OF ALL ITS POWERS OF ACTING AND REASONING AS FEAR.
– EDMUND BURKE[32]

One summer Sue and I took our two children, Matthew and Nicole, on a family vacation that included some time in Switzerland. The country is slightly less than 16,000 square miles, so it's about half the size of South Carolina. But those miles are full of snow-capped mountains, many soaring well above 13,000 feet. There are waterfalls, ice caves, and amazing lakes and valleys. The wine and food are great, and the people are friendly. In short, it's an incredible place to visit.

It was in the Swiss Alps, however, that I had my most dramatic encounter with personal fear.

Our trip took us to Interlaken, a tourist hot-spot because it's a launching pad to the mountains and lakes of the region. It sits along the Aare River between Lake Thun and Lake Brienz ("Interlaken" literally means "between the lakes"), and it offers access to and views of the Jungfrau, Mönch, and Eiger mountains.

As we ate dinner on our first day outside of Interlaken, Matt was engrossed in watching a group of paragliders sail down from the mountains and land in a nearby field. These adrenaline junkies attach a parachute-like canopy to their bodies so they can float on the winds like birds. Rather than jumping from an airplane, they start their ride by running off a cliff and letting the updraft take them soaring into the sky.

These were tandem jumps, so each person was strapped in with a professional paraglider pilot. Matt was a fearless 14-year-old at the time, so you probably can guess what he was thinking.

"Dad," he said after watching a few landings, "let's do this!"

Now, you need to know that I am really afraid of heights. Make that terrified. I don't mind flying in airplanes, but anything that leaves me feeling exposed is big-time trouble. When our family moved to Denver, I couldn't even drive to the top of Pike's Peak.

"There's no way you're going to get me to do that," I told my son.

"Dad, I really want to do it," he said. "Please."

And, so, it continued. He pleaded. I found more and more ways to say the same thing: "No way!" As unrelenting as he was in his desire to paraglide, I was equally unrelenting in my refusal to go.

On our third day there, Sue and I went out for dinner. Matt and Nicole stayed at the hotel, where, again, he watched people paraglide down from the imposing cliffs. We were barely into our salads when he gave me a call.

"Dad, I really want to do it," he said.

I decided I needed to put a stop to this. Matt was a bit of a procrastinator, so I made him a deal that I thought would end the conversation.

"You call and figure it out," I said. "If you make all of the arrangements, I'll do it with you."

I was confident he wouldn't do it, but a few minutes later he called me back.

"It's all booked," he said.

"What do you mean?" I said.

"We meet at 8:30 tomorrow morning, and they take us up the mountain," he said. "Just bring your credit card."

I nearly choked on my wine, but the die was cast.

The next morning, we were on our way to a field that was about 7,000 feet above sea level and 3,000 feet above the landing zone. When we arrived, the pilots went over the basics and then gave us three keys to success:

"One, run as fast as you can toward the edge of the cliff. The updraft will catch you and take you into the air, and the faster you run, the higher you'll go.

"Two, enjoy the most beautiful scenery in the world on the way down.

"And, three, run as fast as you can when we land, or we'll topple over and that might be painful."

Matt listened to the instructions and gave an eager thumbs-up. I asked a million questions until my instructor looked at me and said, "Dude, just don't worry about it."

The four of us—Matt, me, and our pilot-partners—all began running at the same time, but I started to lock up about twenty yards from the edge. The closer we got, the more it felt like I was wearing lead boots and running in deep mud. The instructor was yelling at me, "Run! Run! Run!" I could barely move, and we barely got any lift. Matt, meanwhile, ran like a gazelle and took off like he'd been shot from a cannon.

As we descended, I hardly saw anything. I was so scared that there was no way I could enjoy the scenery. And as we approached the ground, my legs locked up again. Once again, the instructor was yelling, "Run! Run! Run!" And, once again, my body was saying, "No! No! No!" I was barely moving, and I tumbled all over the place. My son, of course, thoroughly enjoyed the flight and nailed his landing.

"Dad, wasn't that really cool?!" Matt said as we came together. And it was. But in my heart and mind I was saying something else: Thank God that's over!

The point, of course, is that I couldn't effectively do all the wise things they told me to do because I was paralyzed by fear. I couldn't properly execute the take-off. I couldn't enjoy the journey. And I couldn't land without bouncing across the ground.

It wasn't a matter of skill. It was a matter of fear.

TACTICS AND EMOTIONS

There's little questioning that fear, whether it's an emotion we experience or a tactic we use, is generally bad for leadership. But not everything about fear is bad.

As a tactic, for instance, fear has a decent track record for achieving immediate results. We tell our kids not to accept Halloween candy from strangers because there may be something harmful in it. The leader of a team might rally her troops by saying the company will lose a client if a deadline is missed. And political candidates say things like, "My opponent will ruin the economy!" Why? Because it works! Indeed, some of the world's most well-known leaders, successful in most of the ways the world defines that word, have a reputation for leading with fear—Mark Pincus of Zynga, Mark Fields of Ford, Rupert Murdoch of News Corp., and Larry Ellison of Oracle, just to name a few. The tactic, of course, works because it plays on the powerful emotion of personal fears.

Simply put, fear is an emotion that's induced by a threat—real or perceived—that you might be harmed (physically, psychologically, emotionally, economically, and so on). There's a section of our brains—the amygdala, or "lizard brain" as it's been labeled—that's programmed to alert us to danger. Sometimes our fears are quite rational and warn us of very real dangers; they encourage us to run from an angry bear, for example. But many things that our brains once rightly classified as dangerous are now simply challenges. That lizard in our heads doesn't always know the difference. It can see all uncertainty as danger, when, in fact, it's often just an inconvenient trial.

When the lizard gets out of control, our fears can become irrational. They are phobias that actually can lead to dizziness, nausea, breathlessness, and, in some cases, panic attacks. In our day-to-day lives, irrational fears play out as insecurities that we try to hide but too often can't fully control. And while they may not always lead to psychological symptoms, they almost always create problems in our relationships with others.

When fears aren't checked by discipline and perspective, they lead to counterproductive thoughts, words, and actions. This can result in passive-aggressive leaders who are overly controlling, intimidating, and manipulative. When those behaviors become a pattern, building trust becomes impossible. And that's why irrational fears—those that don't protect or inspire us—can land us in a world of trouble. When we allow those emotion-based fears to live inside of us and rule over us, we put ourselves in a difficult position, especially in light of the climates we discussed earlier.

Consider, for a minute, the unique ways the realities of our modern world play into our fears and feed our underlying insecurities. If we're not careful, our inner voice soon is whispering things like: *What if technology eliminates the need for my job? What if I can't get along with co-workers who have different political or cultural views? What if I can't keep up with the pace of change? What if I get transferred? What if a competitor buys our company? What if my new boss is twenty years younger than me? What if...?*

Those types of thoughts can lead to common fear-based behaviors that are disastrous to us and to an organization's culture, behaviors such as:

+ Lying to portray beneficial outcomes, perhaps by using social media as a weapon.

+ Hoarding information and maintaining silos inside teams (or between teams) to protect decision-making power.

+ Putting up shields or altering the facts to enhance a carefully constructed perception.

+ Communicating with others only to serve selfish interests rather than to serve the greater good.

+ Staying silent when coworkers gossip about others, tell insensitive jokes, or make derogatory statements.

These types of actions can breed breaches of integrity and a lack of respect for the jobs that others do. And that creates a cancerous situation that can quickly pollute an organization, especially when those behaviors are evident in leaders. Why? Because people watch leaders. They study their behaviors. They make note of what their leaders reward, punish, or ignore. They figure out what it takes to succeed in their environment. Then, in most cases, they consciously or unconsciously alter their behaviors in ways that mirror their leaders in order to fit in and advance.

NAMING OUR LEADERSHIP FEARS

The problem, as I see it, is deeply rooted in the heart of a leader. We all have fears and insecurities. We can't avoid them. But if we search our hearts, we can acknowledge them, name them, and deal with them.

My fear of heights is a mild case of acrophobia, and it's one of more than five hundred phobias you can find in various reference books. The fears and insecurities of a leader typically aren't true phobias—they don't interfere with normal day-to-day life—but they can be extremely harmful, both to the leader and those he or she influences.

These fears take many forms. In my research for this book, I found dozens of descriptions of fears that destroy trust and cripple our influence. But a 2014 survey by Roger Jones of Vantage Hill Partners in London pretty much nailed it for me. After surveying 116 executives and conducting follow-up interviews with twenty-seven of them, Jones put the biggest fears of leaders into five buckets:

1. incompetence

2. underachieving

3. appearing too vulnerable

4. being attacked politically by colleagues

5. looking foolish

Interestingly, all of those fears are about the leaders themselves and how they are perceived, and none are about their organization and how it is performing.

The biggest fear among leaders, according to the research by Jones, is being found to be incompetent—when our insecurities tell us that our reputation as an expert is a farce and that eventually it will somehow be revealed to the world (probably via social media). Externally, we want to project self-confidence. Internally, we know our weaknesses. We see the gap, and we start to worry that others will see it too. The resulting fear is often called the "impostor syndrome," and Jones points out that it, "diminishes (a leader's) confidence and undermines relationships with other executives."[33] I faced these fears the night I passed out during our finance meeting. Not only did I fear being seen as incompetent, I also feared coming across as too vulnerable, all because I wasn't confident I could make the right decisions or provide clear answers.

Leaders who fear they'll be seen as incompetent often don't want to be seen as vulnerable because vulnerability would expose their perceived

LEADERSHIP FEAR BUCKETS

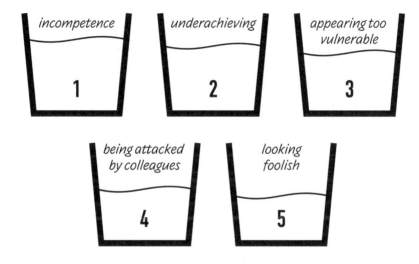

incompetence and, of course, make them look foolish. If vulnerability doesn't expose it, then their underachievement probably will. And if that doesn't, then no doubt it will be exposed by the undermining political attacks of their conniving colleagues, who pounce on demonstrations of vulnerability as a sign of weakness.

You see how these fears feed one another, right?

Dealing with those fears is pretty easy when we're able to think them through rationally and free from pressures or stress. But life is seldom free of pressures or stress. And external forces tend to distract us from what really matters, distort truth, and discourage our hearts.

In today's competitive, fast-paced landscape, for instance, the pressure to keep up can become intense, because each new innovation in technology can threaten our ability to keep pace with the times.

When we worry about our place in the future, we can start worrying about how those five big fears will affect that future. What happens if we're discovered to be less competent than we project, come across as overly vulnerable, get attacked by colleagues who want to advance their personal agenda, or say or do things that make us look foolish? Well, we'll get passed over for promotions or choice assignments, of course. Maybe get laid off. We can't let those things happen, so we give into those fears and allow them to rule our lives and shape our leadership.

FALLOUT OF FEARS

Fears can paralyze leaders or drive them to do all sorts of things they know to be wrong—acting dishonestly, for instance, or tolerating poor behaviors in others when it leads to desired results. In fact, the executives Jones interviewed mentioned more than five hundred negative consequences that resulted from their fear-based dysfunctional behaviors. Those mentioned most frequently include:

+ allowing bad behavior at the next level down,

+ failing to act unless there's a crisis,

+ taking bad risks,

+ being mistrustful and overcautious in relationships with co-workers,

+ and failing to speak up or have honest conversations.[34]

For instance, the fear of underachieving can cause leaders to ignore what I call cultural vipers—those employees whose performance shines but whose cultural fit is askew. They poison the culture with ego but often go unchallenged because a leader fears the potential failure that would follow if the organization lost the immediate performance results the viper delivers. (And, by the way, fears and insecurities also are driving the self-focused behaviors in these vipers.)

When the fear of being seen as incompetent gains momentum, it can snowball to create what Dutch psychologist Manfred F. R. Kets de Vries calls, "neurotic impostors."[35]

"In extreme cases," de Vries writes, "neurotic impostors bring about the very failure that they fear. This self-destructive behavior can take many forms, including procrastination, abrasiveness, and the inability to delegate."[36]

And while the work ethic of these leaders can be contagious, they can also become impatient, harsh, and unrealistic in their expectations, which de Vries says, "inevitably translates into high employee turnover rates, absenteeism, and other complications that can affect the bottom line."[37]

The fear of being attacked politically by colleagues can make leaders distrustful and, in the extremes, paranoid about what others are thinking, saying, or doing behind their backs. These leaders are likely to isolate rather than collaborate or delegate.

And the fear of being seen as too vulnerable or of looking foolish often keeps leaders from saying something they shouldn't say—something offensive, for instance—but it also might cause them to hold blindly to false assumptions about other people rather than asking legitimate questions.

Rather than risk a forced mea culpa from inadvertently saying the wrong thing, many leaders prefer silence. That might be the wise choice in many situations, but silence driven by fear comes with its own set of consequences. Rather than engaging in enlightening conversations, they might take the more comfortable route of spending time mainly in social cliques with people who affirm their views rather than challenging them. Their fear of looking foolish or of coming across as vulnerable, therefore, prevents them from forging relationships that add value to their lives and insights to their business.

In many cases, of course, our fears are unfounded. Our lizard brain is simply confused. And, more often than not, leaders who are over-compensating based on their fears end up doing more harm than good, while leaders who overcome their fears earn trust and see better results. Ian Siegel, co-founder of ZipRecruiter, discovered this truth when he was a twenty-three-year-old manager of a team of veteran engineers at Citysearch, an online guide to cities.

"Four failed CTOs had come before me, and the team was considered difficult and volatile," Siegel said. "I knew they all were smarter than I was, so I told them, 'Just tell me what to do, and I'll do it.'"[38]

In other words, he didn't worry about looking foolish, he didn't worry about looking incompetent, he didn't worry about being vulnerable, he didn't worry about getting credit for the team's achievements, and he didn't worry about office politics. And guess what happened? He earned the respect of a team that previously held its managers in contempt.

A joint study by researchers from Harvard Business School and Wharton School of Business found that someone who seeks advice and input is generally seen as more competent than someone who doesn't. The act of seeking advice requires a sense of intellectual humility that actually can convey wisdom and confidence while providing ego biscuits to the person you are asking to provide help.[39]

Such was the case for Siegel.

"Everyone in the room started immediately telling me that I was the best manager at the company," Siegel said. "The only reason they thought that was because I was the best listener the team had ever had. It sounds so simple, but listening to people is highly effective, especially when you're managing people who are smarter than you."[40]

FACING THE ENEMY

I can relate to all five of the fears outlined by Jones, and I don't know any self-aware leader who can't.

My biggest personal insecurity is being wrong. An executive coach once pointed out that it can make me behave like a perfectionist, and I can be overly demanding of others. Why? I fear failure. I hate to lose—whether it's losing to a competitor or losing a good employee to another company. Failure, according to my insecurities, is proof that I'm incompetent, that I've underachieved, or that I'm foolish. I fear not doing enough or simply not being good enough to win whatever battle I'm facing.

During our efforts to turn things around at Prologis, I battled the particular fear that whatever advantages I had on one day would quickly evaporate the next day. Even the most loyal employees could be enticed to leave overnight. Nothing was forever. Whatever skills I'd acquired, whatever success I'd achieved, it all could be gone in the blink of an eye, and there I would be—looking foolish, feeling vulnerable, and falling short of my goals for myself and for our team.

Fear affects everything we do—whether we're leading a team in a modern organization or paragliding from a cliff in the Swiss Alps. Regardless of which fears you struggle with most or how you label them, I've found the key action item if you want to create transfluence in today's work environments is to look honestly at your fears and admit that they exist. You can't deal with reality until you acknowledge your reality.

When you really boil it down, fear has been a pervasive enemy of leaders since the dawn of time. Access, diversity, and acceleration shape those fears in unique ways and may cause us to respond differently than in ages past. But the root of the problem—fear—is the same. When we look into our hearts, however, we'll find that our fears have a roommate that we also must address: pride. It's the other major storm we need to chase. So, let's take a look at the role pride plays in the hearts of modern leaders. Then we can examine more antidotes to both fears and pride.

CHAPTER RECAP

Fear is one of the two most significant storms a leader must chase. Sometimes fears are effective as a tactic, but most fears are irrational and thwart strong leadership. The fears of most executives relate to themselves and how they are perceived, not their organizations and their people. People watch you as a leader and consciously or subconsciously alter their behaviors in ways that mirror you to fit in. When you are engrossed by your own fears, a number of bad results can happen, including distractions, survival mentality, decision-making paralysis, mistrust, dishonesty, and other dysfunctional behaviors.

TRANSFLUENCE IN ACTION

+ Deal with your fears by naming them one by one. If you can name them, you can deal with them. The most common fears among leaders include incompetence, underachievement, appearing too vulnerable, being politically attacked, and appearing foolish. Do you have similar insecurities?

6.

→ # BIG ME, LITTLE YOU

PRIDE GETS NO PLEASURE OUT OF HAVING SOMETHING, ONLY OUT OF HAVING MORE OF IT THAN THE NEXT MAN.
– C.S. LEWIS[41]

There's a Native American parable about three warriors who make a long and difficult journey to visit a great spirit at a faraway sacred site. They offer the spirit a gift of tobacco, and, in appreciation for the gift, the spirit agrees to grant each of them a wish. One asks for the skills to be a better hunter, "for I have a big family and I'm not able to feed them." His wish is granted. Another asks for a wife, "for I have everything and no one to share it with." His wish also is granted. The third warrior gives the matter some thought and then asks for eternal life, "for I want to live forever." His wish is granted too—he is transformed into a spirit rock!

You've been there, haven't you? Not standing before a spirit offering tobacco in exchange for a wish to be granted, but you've worked hard to get somewhere or to achieve some grand goal and thought, "It's time for the payoff!"

That's when temptation attacks a leader—the temptation of a prideful heart. It's the byproduct of success. It convinces you that you have all the answers, you are the expert, and you deserve the credit. It tells you that you've earned the rewards, and you should get what you want while the getting is good.

A prideful heart feeds your greed and starves your humility. It is filled with self and loses sight of a leader's true purpose—having a transformative influence on the lives of others. Unfortunately, it's often difficult to see before it's too late. We charge forward, driven by our pride until the next thing we know, our hearts are as hard as a spirit rock.

Pride is the other ageless opponent of a transfluent leader, an internal storm that's raged for centuries and across all cultures. More specifically, it's "hubristic pride."

What do I mean by "hubristic pride"?

Many psychologists use two buckets to describe pride. *Authentic pride* comes from feeling confident and productive. It's a good thing. There's nothing wrong with taking pride in our work or feeling pride about things like the accomplishments of our children, our co-workers, or our college football team. *Hubristic pride*, on the other hand, involves vanity, egotism, and arrogance. As psychologist Guy Winch points out, hubristic pride is "related to socially undesirable traits such as being disagreeable, aggressive, having low or brittle self-esteem—and being prone to shame."[42] It's what caused young Narcissus to look into the pool of water and fall in love with the reflection of himself, which is why we have Greek mythology to thank for the term *narcissism*.

Many theologians (across a variety of religions) consider this inwardly directed pride the root of all other sins. It tells us that we are central to everything that's going on around us. If we're focused on getting everything we want, the way that we want it, and in ways that shine the most light on us, then we will refuse to admit our weaknesses, own our mistakes, learn from our errors, or give credit to others who've earned it. Instead, we will boast about what we've done, what we're doing, or what we're planning to do. We will grow defensive when challenged, belittling others to lift ourselves up. And we will serve only one person: ourselves.

William Wilberforce, the English politician and reformer of the late 1700s and early 1800s, saw selfishness at the core of humankind's pride.

"Selfishness is one of the principal fruits of the corruption of human nature," he said, "and it is obvious that selfishness disposes us to over-rate our good qualities and to overlook or extenuate our defects."[43]

We live in a world where social media sites like YouTube can turn just about anyone into a celebrity, where social media "influencer" is a *bona fide* job title, and where the power of the pen has been replaced by the power of the hashtag. Needless to say, our culture often encourages selfish pride and provides the technological vehicles to promote just about anything or anyone quickly and at scale. Unfortunately, author and *New York Times* columnist David Brooks was spot-on when he pointed out that we've developed into a "Big Me" culture.[44] The same social media that provides access and transparency also drives obnoxious amounts of self-promotion and self-glorification.

Hubristic pride destroys good leadership. They simply cannot co-exist together. And, yet, pride is perhaps the most seductive byproduct of successful leadership. Bill Treasurer, chief encouragement officer of Giant Leap Consulting, points out how easy it is for leaders to "slip into the idea that you're better, smarter, and more special" than anyone else. Why? Because the trappings of leadership tell you so.

"First, not everyone gets to be a leader, so the fact that you are one sends the message that there's something special about you," Treasurer says. "Second, leaders get more perks. When you're a leader, you get bigger titles, bigger workspaces, and a bigger salary. Finally, leaders get a lot more behavioral latitude. Nobody challenges you when you show up late for a meeting, interrupt people, or skirt company policies that lower level employees have to abide by."[45]

This leads to inflated egos and the abuse of power. It's an underlying component in almost every leadership scandal.

Remember Martin Shkreli, the former hedge-fund manager who founded Turing Pharmaceutical and quickly rose to a fame worthy of Gordon Gekko? In the summer of 2015, Shkreli's new company bought a fifty-year-old drug and raised the price 5,000 percent in the name of maximizing profits for his investors. The news went viral, and the response to his avarice and arrogant behavior was not kind. Protests were organized, held, recorded, and shared. Web-based sleuths discovered and published Shkreli's phone number and address, opening the floodgates for people to reach out to him personally. Yet, even as he was vilified by social and mainstream media alike, he actively stoked the flames of his public image. *The Wall Street Journal* noted that he posted hours of streaming online videos of himself "playing chess, strumming the guitar and answering questions from strangers."[46] He also used social media to boast of his romantic prowess, defend his business decisions, and mock presidential candidates.[47]

For another example of hubristic pride run amok, consider the FBI's investigation of FIFA, the world governing body for soccer. Fourteen people were indicted on forty-seven charges ranging from racketeering to wire

PR⭡DE

"PRIDE RESULTS FROM OVERVALUING OURSELVES AND UNDERVALUING OTHERS."

JOHN MACARTHUR

fraud to money laundering. The group's powerful president, Sepp Blatter, begrudgingly resigned in 2015, just four days after he was re-elected. Michael Hershman, who was a member of the Independent Governance Committee working with FIFA on reforms, described the organization's leadership culture as arrogant. "There are people in decision making at FIFA that are arrogant and believe FIFA should answer to no one, that they are above the law," Hershman said at the time. "That absolutely needs to change."[48]

One of the most compelling story lines of 2017 involved women coming forward to bring light to the centuries-old problem of sexual harassment. Titans in the entertainment, news, business, sports, and political arenas all found themselves suddenly held accountable for wrongful behaviors that resulted at least in part due to their hubristic pride.

Pride of this type comes with at least two realities. The first, as theologian John MacArthur points out, is that it never satisfies. "Pride results from overvaluing ourselves and undervaluing others," MacArthur notes. "It leads to restlessness because it makes us dissatisfied with what we have and concerned about what everyone else is doing. It keeps us always hungering for more attention and adoration."[49]

The second reality is that it creates leadership blind spots. It prevents leaders from seeing their personal weaknesses and the weaknesses of their

PRIDE CREATES LEADERSHIP BLIND SPOTS.

organizations. All too often, this causes leaders to practice the ancient arts of justification and denial. They have a blind eye and a deaf ear to the realities around them, and they isolate rather than embrace any wise counsel that might come their way. Most of us don't like to be wrong, and we especially don't like to admit to others when we're wrong. So, we put up walls, or we offer excuse after excuse for what went wrong rather than looking for legitimate reasons and taking personal responsibility for our mistakes. We close our minds to truth and forget about doing what's right because we're focused on protecting our image. Then, rather than building on our successes, we put ourselves and our entire organization at risk.

When pride (and fear) become pervasive in the leadership ranks, leaders stop listening to others. They have a hard time giving up control. They seldom express how they feel in transparent ways. People throughout the organization, meanwhile, develop victim mentalities. Fingers are pointed, blame is cast in every direction but inward, and a lack of accountability often becomes a hallmark of the culture. People are afraid to take responsibility and can become too insecure to speak up—for themselves or for others. They begin thinking and working in silos and are sometimes immune to critically important things going on in other areas of the organization. They might be great individually but operate on their own little islands.

ORGANIZATIONAL ARROGANCE

You might see pride as a flaw that primarily reflects back on the individual. A leader who is overdosing on vanity, in other words, is only hurting himself or herself. But pride soaks into a culture the way paint soaks into a brush, and pretty soon it re-colors everything around it.

Look at any organization around the globe that's been faced with the challenge of rebuilding a broken trust, and you'll likely see an unfortunate byproduct of its earlier success: organizational arrogance.

You know the story: An organization experiences success. It takes that success for granted in some quarters and arrogance blooms. Trust is broken, and success begins to unravel.

Examples? Well, there's the Roman Empire, of course. But how about something more recent?

PRIDE SOAKS INTO A CULTURE THE WAY PAINT SOAKS INTO A BRUSH, AND PRETTY SOON IT RE-COLORS EVERYTHING AROUND IT.

Remember Volkswagen and its software designed to fool regulators about emissions?

Chris Wright, a journalist who writes about business and finance for *Forbes*, was a Volkswagen owner, so he had firsthand experience with how the company interacted with customers on the emissions scandal. In a blog for *Forbes*, Wright described the arrogant attitude he perceived in the first letter he received from the company. The letter, Wright said, took an almost clinical approach. It informed him that his car was "affected by this issue," and it offered no apologies.

"The tone of the whole thing—my first direct communication, as an owner, from Volkswagen since their 'emissions issue'—is of someone discussing an unforeseen mechanical glitch," Wright said, "one of those things that just happens from time to time, as opposed to a deliberate attempt to sabotage emissions testing in order to continue to pollute the environment beyond acceptable levels, all for corporate profit. 'Emissions issue?' Seriously? That's like saying Lance Armstrong had a 'testing issue.' Volkswagen cheated everyone: regulators, the environment, us."[50]

Ed Whitacre is another executive who once found himself in a culture that, in my opinion, had some serious pride issues. Whitacre was appointed CEO of General Motors in 2009 in the wake of the government bailout of the company. He vividly recalls what he heard when he arrived and began asking leaders about the reasons for the company's financial troubles.

"I got an earful about how the collapse wasn't their fault," Whitacre wrote in *American Turnaround*. "It was due to some combination of bad luck, bad timing, and bad circumstances. In other words, bad management had nothing to do with it. 'The economy got us,' one executive told me. His comment stayed with me, like gum on the bottom of a shoe. I will always remember that quote."

Organizational arrogance might not be the only thing such problem-plagued organizations have in common, but it's certainly near the top of the list. Business. Sports. Politics. Academia. Nonprofits. This year. Last year. Next year. Every year. There's no shortage of examples of how hubristic pride in individual leaders results in organizational arrogance that can rot otherwise great organizations at their core. And, as I think I've made clear, Prologis was right there among them when I found myself returning as CEO. We were like a diseased oak tree that looked strong and mighty on the outside, but that was sick and weakening on the inside.

THE DILEMMA

Let me give you an example of something that happened to me prior to becoming CEO that wreaked havoc on my job and, ultimately, wreaked havoc across the management ranks of our organization. It was driven by fears and pride, and it's something I now refer to now as "the dilemma."

Prologis more than tripled in size between 2004 and 2007, growing from about $11 billion in assets to more than $36 billion. That might sound impressive, but most of our growth was not organic. Instead, it was largely fueled by acquisitions of other assets and companies. Now, admittedly, some of that growth was driven by market-based opportunities at somewhat reasonable prices. But much of it was fueled by a fear that if we didn't buy the target company, a competitor would. It was pure paranoia, lacking real discipline, and fueled by a high-growth mindset that's common in a fast-paced business world where change is omnipresent. In many cases, we overpaid for the right to buy what we desperately wanted, all for the sake of growth—and our shareholders eventually paid dearly for it.

The struggle over the price we were paying for our growth was just one of a host of issues where there was massive disagreement among the management team. When that happens, leaders at the top can feel vulnerable, and when they feel vulnerable, they often do everything in their power to prove their worth. They come to work with their armor on and their spear in hand, ready to fight anyone with a different view of the business than their own and too proud to concede even an inch of ground. Their fear of being second guessed can lead them to becoming heavy-handed, dictatorial, arrogant, or non-communicative. Their pride typically causes them to revert to command-and-control leadership methods, and they usually lose sight of one of the most important aspects of their role—to humbly recognize their weaknesses and listen to others.

That was our environment in 2007 when our CEO orchestrated a deal to buy a competitor in the United Kingdom. He flew to Bermuda, met with the CEO of the other company, and agreed to pay about $750 million for the acquisition. Most of us had no idea he was even in serious discussions with them, so we were all shocked to learn about the deal. The closer we looked at the details of the transaction, however, the more we saw what we all feared: the numbers didn't add up.

Our evaluation of the deal was ugly. First of all, our existing European team wanted no part of the acquired company. There were serious personality issues and some bad blood between our leaders in Europe and the leaders of the company we were buying. What's more, our best estimate of the company's value was $500 million. I don't know what world you live in financially, but we saw that as a significant gap! In the eyes of the management team, we were overpaying by at least $250 million. Our most optimistic estimates of the yield from future cash flows of the business were still well below our cost of capital, which was the most important yardstick in sizing up the profitability of every acquisition.

An acquisition of this size needed the approval of our board. It was important we all got on the same page before asking for that approval, so a few of us took our concerns to our CEO. When the question was raised as to how he arrived at a higher value, our CEO responded by telling us that the acquisition was too important to lose and that we needed to "get on board" because it was "imperative that we make the deal." He also told me, in no uncertain terms, that he expected my full support as a fellow board member. In other words, no matter my misgivings, he expected my vote when the board met.

Can you imagine how I felt? As the president and COO, I wanted to support our CEO and promote harmony within the management team. But as a board member, it was my job—in fact, my fiduciary duty—to vote on behalf of our shareholders. In this case, I was being asked to vote against my conscience and, therefore, not appropriately exercise my duty. And because of the heavy-handed way it was dealt with, neither I nor the team felt like our opinions were valued. In fact, we felt as if a gun were to our head to do the wrong thing.

Nothing was transparent about the process or the solution. And this lack of transparency only further eroded our trust as a team. Effectively, I felt obligated to lie to the board about my true feelings. In doing so, I'd be lying to myself, to the rest of the leadership team, and to our shareholders. We were in a box. I was in a box. And it was all due to fear and pride—the fear of losing an acquisition to a competitor and pride that says, I'm the smartest guy in the room, and I don't need to listen to anyone else. Frankly, in this case, our CEO was dead-set on making the deal himself, so he never asked our opinions in advance or told us anything about it. And that's what created the dilemma.

As I wrestled with my circumstance, I knew I had to deal with my own pride and fears. Were my personal fears and my wounded pride clouding my view of the deal? Or were they tempting me to avoid confrontation and the inevitable fallout that would come from it?

My decision would impact far more than whether we acquired another company. If I gave into our CEO and supported the deal, I would lose a measure of self-respect. And a "no" vote would certainly add to the ongoing tension in the ranks of the executive team. That type of tension typically ends up fatal to someone's job—and, in this case, it would likely be mine.

FROM PRIDE AND FEARS TO TRUST

I'll tell you the specifics later of how I handled that dilemma and the fallout that surrounded it, but first we need to discuss the broader hard truth: If we can't get past our fears and insecurities, we'll never overcome our hubristic pride and build the trust we need to energize and engage people with transformative influence. Thus, we will either create dilemmas for those around us, or we'll struggle to lead well when we face the inevitable dilemmas that test us.

Instead, we need to create an environment where leaders learn to place their trust in others and, in doing so, build trust in their spheres of influence. When leaders learn to trust themselves and place their trust in others, they take the first steps in building widespread transfluence. But trust isn't handed out with college diplomas. It doesn't come with the keys to the corner office. It has to be earned, and, once earned, maintained. Any break in consistency— or even a perceived break in consistency—is shared at lightning speed with multiple audiences.

Earning trust, keeping trust, and sharing trust are all essential to modern leadership, and it doesn't happen when we are overwhelmed by the negative aspects of access, acceleration, and diversity. It happens when we counter those climates with a strong microclimate that shapes who we are as a leader and how we respond to our dilemmas.

CHAPTER RECAP

Pride is the other significant storm a leader must face. Authentic pride comes from feeling confident and productive and can be a good thing. Hubristic pride, on the other hand, involves vanity, egotism, and arrogance. It is perhaps the most seductive byproduct of leadership. It's a leadership killer.

TRANSFLUENCE IN ACTION

+ Put your pride on the shelf when you lead. Build a strong microclimate that shapes who you are as a leader and enables you to withstand the storms of pride that corrupt trust and get in the way of having a transformative influence on others.

PART III: CREATING A MICROCLIMATE

DEEP ROOTS ARE NOT REACHED BY THE FROST.

– J.R.R. TOLKIEN[51]

TRANSFLUENT LEADERS CREATE A STRONG MICROCLIMATE BY DEVELOPING THREE PRACTICES:

*Look outside
the storms*   *Embrace
transparency*   *Act authentically
through a 3H-Core*

The brick, concrete, and asphalt in some cities absorb and re-radiate so much of the sun's energy that it creates urban heat islands—pockets where the climate is markedly different from the surrounding areas. These types of microclimates also form naturally, like within a cave or around a body of water.

Most of us live at the mercy of the climates around us. Yet, as leaders, we all have a responsibility to build a strong microclimate to protect us against those climates and enable us to live out a broader purpose—to have a transformative influence in the lives of others—regardless of the circumstances.

If our leadership microclimate is marked by fear and hubristic pride, our influence becomes poisonous. Transfluent leaders create a strong microclimate by developing three practices that destroy pride, defeat fears, and set them up for success. This kind of microclimate exists when we: focus our attention on others, allow the world to clearly see who we are, and live our values through our actions.

In other words, when we: look outside of our storms, embrace transparency, and act authentically through what I call a 3H-Core.

Let's look at what that entails.

GUIDEPOST NO. 4

SELFISHNESS IS OUR DEFAULT RESPONSE AS HUMANS.

BE SELFLESS AND DIFFERENT.

7.

LOOKING OUTSIDE OUR STORMS

WHO IS THE HAPPIEST OF MEN? HE WHO VALUES THE MERITS
OF OTHERS, AND IN THEIR PLEASURE TAKES JOY, EVEN AS
THOUGH 'TWERE HIS OWN.
– JOHANN WOLFGANG VON GOETHE[52]

Willie Cook walked into the small grocery store my family owned in the Herron Hill District of Pittsburgh and gathered several inexpensive items into a shopping bag—four cartons of cigarettes, a can of room deodorant, a tube of toothpaste, and some food.

He walked to the register and asked my dad to make change for a twenty-dollar bill. Then, as Dad counted the change, Cook took a lye solution he had mixed in a coffee can, threw it into my father's face, and raced toward the door with $18 worth of unpurchased goods.

Dad grabbed the closest thing to him—a bottle of syrup—and threw it at Cook, breaking the bottle and cutting Cook's head as Cook fled. Cook was arrested fifteen minutes later and eventually pled guilty to his crimes, but his assault had left my father in a serious condition.

"There's nothing more vicious than the throwing of acid or lye in a person's eye," the judge would tell Cook at the sentencing. "You would have been better off using a gun."[53]

It was May 26, 1960, and I was still just two years old as my mother and grandmother rushed to the emergency room of St. Francis General Hospital to await word on my father's fate. My dad, who was thirty at the time, suffered burns on his face, neck, shoulder, and elbow, but the most severe injury was

A FUNDAMENTAL TRUTH ABOUT TRANSFORMATIVE INFLUENCE: IT'S NOT ABOUT YOU.

the burn to his eyes. For several days, in fact, my parents feared the attack would leave my father completely blind.

"Every day we prayed with each other that he would be able to see you again," my mother told me when she would recount the story.

Fortunately, Dad's right eye healed enough that he could see with the aid of glasses, which also helped cover the disfigurations on his face. And eventually his sight in that eye improved. The other eye, however, was replaced with an egg-shaped piece of glass.

Clearly my parents faced some pretty significant challenges in the immediate aftermath of his injuries, and their fears weighed heavily on their minds. What if my dad lost his sight completely? How long might he be out of work? Or limited in his work? How would he react to suspicious customers? How might this change his view of people, including himself?

Dad could have second-guessed how he handled the robbery and allowed that blow to his pride to grow into an insecurity about his ability to take care of the store—and his family. He could have grown fearful of how other people might judge him because of the burn marks around his eyes. He could have grown bitter, angry, defiant, and distrustful. He could have isolated himself from people or treated everyone around him as another potential assailant.

Instead, my dad faced his pride and fears in a different way: by taking the focus off of himself.

My dad recognized a fundamental truth about transformative influence: it's not about you.

Of course, he never described his outlook as a key element in a strong leadership microclimate. But when I reflect on his life, it's easy to see how his outward focus shaped his influence—on me and on everyone who knew him. He didn't wallow in self-pity. He served others—his wife, his family, his customers, his friends, and his community. He wasn't happy about what had happened to him, but he wasn't bitter about it. Instead, he was thankful that he had survived and grateful for more time with the people who were around him. Rather than looking into his fears and pride and allowing them to shape his future around all that he had lost, he kept his sights squarely on all that he had and all that he could give to others. That outward focus was part of who he was, and it was a reason he stood out in the storms of his life.

When we get up every morning, we can choose to focus on the fears and pride within us. Giving them our attention gives them permission to influence, and at times even rule, our decisions. They become the storm-makers of our microclimate.

Think about this in the context of the three big climates we've discussed throughout this book. If we're focused inwardly on our pride and fear, our decisions about access, acceleration, and diversity become self-serving. Technology becomes a tool we use to access information for our own purposes. We see the speed of change and diverse opinions as enemies—threats to our positions of power and our paths to success. We become preoccupied with what we want and the things we think we need to protect us or to advance our personal agendas.

The better choice is to look outside of ourselves, which gives us a full view of the climates, good and bad, and puts the storms into the context of a bigger, more hope-filled reality. Access to information and diverse opinions become tools for driving collaboration and meaningful change. We use social media to inspire and equip others, not to argue with others, to demean their points of view, or over-emphasize the highlights of our lives. We see technology as something we can use to help others excel in their work and lead more fulfilling lives, not as a threat to our job security. We see the value of making quick and timely decisions, without feeling threatened by a false need to make premature decisions. And if we're not consumed by our fears and pride, we're free to give proper attention to the things that the fast pace of life can truly threaten—things like rest and work-life balance.

Modern leadership comes with a tremendous need to focus our attention on those we lead—in other words, to serve others. The diverse congregations we serve demand our attention, and many of them will hashtag us into submission if we ignore them for too long. The ability to focus outside ourselves, however, isn't just about paying attention to the various viewpoints of others, and it certainly isn't something we should do because it's forced upon us. Instead, it starts with an inner confidence. So, if we want a microclimate that helps us look outside the storms of life, then we have to lead with an inner confidence. We need a sense of security that thwarts our fears and provides a degree of certainty in our interactions with others.

DEALING WITH THE UNKNOWN

H.P. Lovecraft, who achieved fame posthumously for his horror fiction writing, once said that "the oldest and strongest emotion of mankind is fear, and the oldest and strongest kind of fear is fear of the unknown."[54] Well said. But a blog by Steve Gilbert opened my mind to something even more profound: the unknown isn't what really scares us; what we project into the unknown is the true cause of our anxieties. That hit me like a ton of bricks, because it told me fear is not out of my control. Rather, it is within my control if I can project positive outcomes into the blank space called the unknown.

The solution, of course, lies in what you project. And the more certainty you put into the unknown blank space, the better, because we all crave certainty.

Deep within the nearly six hundred pages of the Six Sigma Leadership Handbook, you'll find an interesting discussion on change leadership that stresses the importance of certainty.

"At its core, leadership is about creating conditions of increased certainty in the present and confidence in the possibility of a much better future," the handbook says. "Leadership in this sense is an affective endeavor targeting doubt and fear and transforming them into confidence and hope. Leadership is that constellation of behaviors that enables an individual or group of individuals to continually act with more confidence and hope in the face of uncertainty and threat in order to create a desired future."[55]

Science backs this up. David Rock, director of the NeuroLeadership Institute and author of Your Brain at Work, points out that, "Uncertainty registers [in the brain] ... as an error, gap, or tension: something that must be corrected before one can feel comfortable again. That is why people crave certainty."[56]

Certainty actually releases chemicals in the brain that lead to positive feelings. Uncertainty releases chemicals that produce a threat response. At its core, uncertainty is rooted in fear. They go together like salad and dressing. Certainty, on the other hand, requires an inner sense of security. It projects a confidence that can't be shaken by circumstances. And it is rooted in the wisdom that outcomes may not always be what you want, but the journey will produce better long-term results.

One of the ways we create a sense of certainty is by listening to and relying on others. It can be dangerous to just listen to ourselves. Instead, we have to open ourselves up to what others have to say. In doing so, we not only create a more well-rounded view of our circumstances, but we also serve them by trusting them to play their parts in our collective success. You hear a lot about the importance of believing in yourself, and self-confidence is an important quality. But if you trust primarily in your own abilities, eventually it will feed your pride rather than help you conquer your fears and insecurities. If you combine your self-confidence with a reliance on things like your team, your experiences, your processes, your well-thought-out strategies, your friends, your family, and your interactions with others, then you're creating a microclimate that allows you to lead with more certainty and at the same time serve the needs of those you lead, extending trust across your organization. If your focus is on the people you serve, and they feel empowered to act, the results ultimately will be far better in the long run. You will establish trust, and people will fight for the opportunity to work with you.

How many times have you seen a manager take on a task because he wasn't confident his subordinate would reach the right answer or achieve the desired result? The manager is projecting a possible mistake into his blank space called the unknown, and it stokes his fears. So, he does the job instead to make sure the outcome is right. How does that work out? Well, in the short run, probably fine. But in the long run, there's a good chance it tarnishes trust in their relationship. The focus, of course, is on the manager as opposed to how the manager could help improve their subordinate's performance.

FLIPPING THE PYRAMID

Frank Blake's early tenure as CEO of Home Depot provides a great example of what it looks like to focus outside of ourselves and empower others throughout an organization. Frank is first and foremost a man who appreciates people and thinks more about them than he does himself. In the organizational chart, he puts them above him—literally. Let me explain.

Blake is a lawyer by training, and he worked in private practice and for the government before going to work for General Electric and eventually handling mergers and acquisitions for Jack Welch. He went to Home Depot in 2002 and helped build the non-retail parts of its business before the board of directors asked him to become CEO around the start of 2007. It wasn't a job he had aspired to have, so he had to make some quick adjustments when he began leading more than 350,000 associates spread across thousands of stores.

One of his first challenges was to go on the company's internal television network and present himself and his vision as their new leader. Blake had never given a speech like this to an audience this large. But since he had worked for some great leaders, including three US presidents, he wasn't shy in front of a microphone, and he didn't lack for confidence. He easily could have sat down in front of the camera and told those associates how things would change under his leadership. Instead, he recognized his need for help as he tapped into his desire to say what the associates needed to hear and not just what he wanted to tell them.

As he thought through what he should communicate and how, he turned for guidance to his son, who had gone to work for Home Depot a few years earlier and was managing a store in Colorado when Blake became CEO. His son didn't tell him what to say, but he mentioned that he routinely started his store meetings by reading from Built from Scratch, a book by the company's

INVERTED PYRAMID

Source: *Built from Scratch* by Bernie Marcus and Arthur Blank

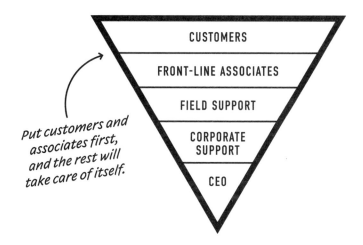

Put customers and associates first, and the rest will take care of itself.

CUSTOMERS

FRONT-LINE ASSOCIATES

FIELD SUPPORT

CORPORATE SUPPORT

CEO

founders. So, Blake read the book in search of inspiration, and he found it on the pages that describe the inverted pyramid organizational model. In this model, the CEO and other executives are on the bottom, and the front-line associates and customers are at the top. The approach perfectly represented Blake's values and view of servant leadership.

"That's what I'm gonna read," he decided.

He did, and the next thing he knew, inverted pyramids were popping up in Home Depot break rooms all across the country. The more he thought about the value of flipping the pyramid, the more it became the key model for his leadership style. When I talked to Blake about the lessons he's learned about leadership, he pointed out examples of why he values the inverted pyramid, and all of them aligned with the principles of transfluence. Here are four that stuck with me:

1. It underscores the importance of integrity.

Leaders are in a weight-bearing position, so they have to be strong. Not physically, although that might help, but pillars of strength because of their integrity. They need to be trusted. "And if you've got fractured loyalties," he said, "if you're self-dealing or dealing for something other than the common good, you're going to split. ... The organization fractures without integrity."

2. It recognizes that the important stuff happens above you.

With the pyramid flipped, the bulk of an organization's customer-facing and/or product producing workforce is placed at the top—above those who supervise. When that happens, leaders realize there is no room for pride. They need to cater their attention to those handling the more important stuff.

3. It's all uphill.

When you see yourself at the bottom of the inverted pyramid, Blake told me, you recognize that the forces of gravity aren't your friends. Rather than climbing to the top and enjoying the view, you're doing the hard work of pushing things up to the masses and away from you.

4. It's centered on others.

This point brings it all together. You simply can't focus on yourself if you're truly going to operate in support of others from a weight-bearing position, treat others in ways that honor them for doing the important stuff, and willingly do the hard work that comes with the uphill climb of serving others. And it creates more certainty in your decisions because they are based on a more well-rounded view. You still have to make hard decisions that others might disagree with, but even those are done with the best interests of others at heart.

These four realities have a huge impact on communication, especially in larger organizations. In fact, Blake believes any organization with more than about thirty employees has scaled to the point that one-on-one communication isn't always an option. When you need to communicate uphill to the people who are doing the most important work, you can't write a memo and think that it automatically will cascade throughout the organization.

"Your message has to work up through osmosis," he said.

When you think about it that way, you realize the message must be simple enough that people can comprehend it quickly, and it's got to be something they can easily relate to and share in their own personal way. "It's got to be consistent or otherwise it gets lost as it moves up," he said.

One of the best ways to do this is by connecting to the self-interests of associates through stories. Those stories, told in simple, relatable ways with consistent language, get repeated and reinforced.

The same approach applies to listening, but in reverse. If you embrace the idea that everything important happens above you, then you recognize the need to listen to the needs of the people on the front lines. But getting people to speak transparently and honestly about their challenges isn't easy.

"Very few people are stupid enough to think their career in any organization is made by raising their hand and telling the boss that something's not going right," Blake told me. "Everybody has figured out the best way to deal with the boss is to tell him or her that they are awesome and everything is great."

To overcome that reality, you have to become an "aggressive listener." That doesn't happen from behind a desk, and it doesn't happen by walking the front lines and asking questions like, How's it going?

"If that's your notion of a question and listening," Blake said, "you're not going to hear anything, because the answer is always, 'Everything's great, boss. You're wonderful. Leave me alone.'"

Aggressive listening requires consistent, authentic actions—a leader has to be intentional about seeking people who know what's going on, asking thoughtful questions, not settling for shallow answers, demonstrating a caring attitude, affirming what they've heard, and following through on promises that are made. You can't do that if your fears and pride are in control. You can only do that if you are looking outside your storms and focusing on others.

DON'T LEAD LIKE SHEEP

We live in a post-agrarian society, so most of us have very little real-world experience tending sheep. I've seen sheep in fields and in petting zoos, but I've never actually cared for them as a shepherd. I'm guessing you haven't either. But here are a few things I do know about sheep—they are stubborn, skittish, smelly, and downright stupid. Oh, yeah, one more thing: we all can be like sheep at times.

We need the certainty found in a strong, caring shepherd—a leader with an inner confidence and a sense of security that comes from looking outside his or her storms and, in doing so, conquers fears and deals with the blank spaces of our unknowns. That's the courage of a shepherd.

In Long Walk to Freedom, Nelson Mandela wrote about the trials he experienced when pushing South Africa forward. Despite those trials, which included twenty-seven years in prison, he led with certainty and courage. He never was imprisoned by his inner storms, and he inspired others to live and lead outside the storms that might otherwise cause them to cower like sheep.

"I learned that courage was not the absence of fear, but the triumph over it," he wrote. "The brave man is not he who does not feel afraid, but he who conquers that fear."[57]

How did he conquer fear? Well, one way was by looking outside himself and focusing on the greater cause of serving others. When Mandela was released in 1990, he didn't lament his sufferings, beat his chest proudly because of the things he had accomplished as an anti-apartheid advocate, or demand attention or rewards. Instead, he reaffirmed his approach to shepherd leadership.

"I stand here before you not as a prophet but as a humble servant of you, the people," he said as he opened his remarks before a crowd in Cape Town. "Your tireless and heroic sacrifices have made it possible for me to be here today. I therefore place the remaining years of my life in your hands."[58]

Transfluent leaders like Mandela create an inner microclimate that allows them to overcome their fears and pride and focus on others by courageously looking outside their storms. But they don't stop there. They also allow people to look into their hearts and really see who they are as leaders, which is the next key to creating your microclimate.

CHAPTER RECAP

The first step in building your microclimate is to look outside the storms of fear and pride that exist within all of us. Fear and pride are driven by selfish thinking. Transfluent leadership is driven by selfless thinking. Selfless thinking requires an inner confidence supported by a sense of security that provides a degree of certainty in your interactions with others. Certainty is determined by what you project into your unknown future. You influence your thinking based on what you project, positively or negatively.

TRANSFLUENCE IN ACTION

+ Control your fear and insecurities by projecting certainty and positive outcomes into the blank space called the unknown.

+ Think selflessly by considering and relying on others in the decisions you make.

+ Try putting yourself at the bottom of an inverted pyramid when it comes to realizing where important stuff happens. Your message as a leader will defy the forces of gravity.

GUIDEPOST NO. 5

TRANSPARENCY IS SCARY
AND UNCOMFORTABLE.

BE BOLD AND LET PEOPLE IN.

8.

 # EMBRACING TRANSPARENCY

THE CURRENCY OF LEADERSHIP IS TRANSPARENCY.
– HOWARD SCHULTZ, CEO OF STARBUCKS[59]

There's a remote region in northern China called the Jiuzhaigou Valley. According to legend, this spectacular valley formed when a jealous devil caused a beautiful goddess to drop a mirror made of wind. The mirror, a gift from her true love, shattered into more than a hundred pieces. The shards of glass formed lakes and ponds that now provide some of the most beautifully transparent waters in the world.

The hillsides of the Min Mountains fold down into pools like Wuhua Hai (Five Flower Lake), Jing Hai (Mirror Lake), and Wucai Chi (Five-Color Pond). The gentle waters are so crystal clear, you can easily see the ancient fallen trees or vibrantly colored underwater landscapes at the bottom.[60]

It's an ecosystem of transparency.

On the other side of the world, another legend holds that the "Peacemaker" once brought together leaders from five warring tribal nations—the Seneca, Cayuga, Onondaga, Oneida, and Mohawk. Along the shores of Onondaga Lake just northwest of modern-day Syracuse, NY, the leaders agreed to put down their arms and formed the Haudenosaunee Confederacy—which claims to be the first representative democracy in the Western world.

For generations, the tranquil waters of Onondaga Lake were considered sacred, but the confederacy lost control of the area following the American Revolutionary War. Resorts dotted the 4.6-mile shoreline during the 19th Century, and the lake remained known for its beauty. Urbanization and industrialization soon began to take a toll, however, and sewage and industrial waste eventually polluted the once hallowed water. Ice harvesting was banned in 1901. Swimming was outlawed in 1940. And mercury contamination climbed so high that fishing was banned in 1970. It was widely regarded as the most polluted lake in America until a lawsuit led to a $700 million cleanup that took nearly thirty years to complete.[61]

It was an ecosystem in distress.

These two vastly different bodies of water—Onondaga Lake and those throughout the Jiuzhaigou Valley—provide an interesting metaphor for leadership. More and more, the world demands an ecosystem of transparency from its leaders. It demands something like the Jiuzhaigou Valley. Yet despite many valiant attempts to create this utopia, the hearts of many leaders typically look far more like the polluted waters of Onondaga Lake. The waters are muddy and murky, contaminated by fears and pride. The ecosystem is in distress. There's a lack of transparency. And when there's a lack of transparency, there's not much trust.

Transparency, as it turns out, is not just a reality that modern leaders face in a high-speed, open-access world—it's also part of the solution to our fears and hubristic pride. It's part of the microclimate we need to create as leaders. Yes, we live in glass houses, but by creating an environment with greater transparency, we naturally prevent ourselves from hiding behind our pride and burying our fears.

IN PURSUIT OF TRANSPARENCY

Developing a microclimate of personal transparency isn't easy. It requires the confidence to know that opening ourselves up won't somehow bring about the end of the world (or even the end of our worlds). We have to let go of some things we don't want to give up because we fear what life might be like without them or because we're conditioned to value control. Many of us live with clenched fists rather than open hands. We struggle to acknowledge that our pride and insecurities even exist, much less embrace our need to know them.

When we are truly transparent as leaders—when we open ourselves up to others—it provides a balance to our personal biases, experiences, and beliefs. It lets in objectivity and outside points of view. Developing this type

DEVELOPING TRANSPARENCY: THE FIRST STEP IS TO GATHER INPUT AND DEVELOP YOURSELF IN THREE CRITICAL WAYS.

measurement   *mentorship*   *mindset*

of transparency is a process that involves time, focus, and effort. It won't happen, however, unless you are transparent with yourself. This requires you to gather input and develop yourself in three critical ways. I call them measurement, mentorship, and mindset.

1. Measurement: A Baseline of Self-awareness

Transparency begins with understanding yourself. What is it that you do well and what are your insecurities? But, as author Ronnie Floyd aptly noted, that type of authentic self-awareness is not easy in today's world.

"Talking about authenticity does not mean authenticity is taking place," Floyd wrote in Living Fit. "With the barrage of information you face each day due to the ubiquity of social media, truth about anything—including yourself—is difficult to evaluate."

In fact, very few leaders can spot their issues on their own. That's why I'm a big believer in seeking professional help. I strongly believe in the benefits gained in hiring an executive coach to help you develop a baseline of self-awareness.

Many leaders, of course, aren't open to receiving feedback from a coach or anyone else. As their success grows, so does their self-confidence. Before they know it, their faith resides mainly in their own opinions. They are more prone to poor decisions, and they promote a culture that devalues collaboration and transparency. The best leaders, however, recognize the value of executive coaching. Ray Williams, in an article for Psychology Today, notes that CEOs such as Eric Schmidt (Google), Jonathan Schwartz (formerly with Sun Microsystems), Steve Bennett (formerly with Intuit), and William Johnson (H.J. Heinz) all used and valued executive coaches.[62]

In a separate article, Johnson told author John Kador that great CEOs are like great athletes, so they "benefit from coaches that bring a perspective that comes from years of knowing [you], the company and what [you] need to do as CEO to successfully drive the company forward. Every CEO can benefit from strong, assertive and honest coaching."[63]

Executive coaches don't have to be expensive. You don't have to work in the C-suite to benefit from an executive coach or afford one. A good place to start is to hire someone to administer some basic evaluation tools like personality or strengths testing and 360-degree evaluations. Assessments like DiSC, StengthsFinder, and the Strengths Deployment Inventory are proven methods for helping you develop self-awareness. A 360-assessment will tell you how you view yourself in relation to how others view you. This will help you spot gaps and create a development plan to address your weaknesses and improve your strengths. It also helps you understand who you really are, not just who you think you are, because it is objective and brings forth the insights of others who know you.

As CEO, I made sure everyone on our senior management team was tested, evaluated, and coached. In retrospect, I wish I would have instituted a similar policy deeper into the organization.

Over the years, this process has taught me a lot about myself. Some lessons have been easier to digest than others. I have learned, for example, that as a leader I can be impatient and too quick to decide on certain things. I have been told I create standards for myself and others that are viewed as unrealistic. And I was once told I needed to slow down and spend more time with people...that in the eyes of my direct reports I appeared too busy for them to feel comfortable enough to take up my time. In other words, I needed to place more emphasis on empathy and less on crowding my schedule with more meetings.

Frankly, sometimes transparency is tough. In my case, it's still not easy to hear negative things about myself. But by acknowledging my weaknesses, I'm better prepared. I'm insecure about far fewer things. Instead, I can have confidence that the best decisions I will make as a leader are those that involve the counsel of others, aren't knee-jerk responses, and are realistic in the eyes of those I lead.

2. Mentorship: A Personal Gut Check

The next step in the journey of greater transparency is having the willingness to "expose" your issues rather than "enclose" them. This requires a willingness to share those issues with others who are closest to you. An executive coach is great, but the most transparent leaders I know also have a mentor, an "accountability" team, a personal board of directors, or some combination of those groups. These are the people who get the most direct and unfiltered views into your heart, because they are the most qualified to help you shape what they see there.

You might have mentors who advise you specifically on work and career-related matters, but I believe you also need mentors who know you on a deep, personal level—your fears, your hopes, your dreams, your beliefs...everything. These mentors may or may not help you make a key business decision, but they most certainly will help you approach the decision in ways that are true to what you believe and how you want to live.

Whatever form it takes, these mentors are friends you trust who will help you define your core values, tell you the hard truth you need to hear, and hold you accountable to living and leading better each day, each week, and each year.

I personally meet regularly with two accountability groups that consist of some of my best friends. We can talk about almost anything in our lives, because we know each other well and trust each other deeply. Being able to verbalize our issues and obtain feedback from those who know us best is a critical component to building transparency that filters out to everyone else in our lives.

3. Mindset: A Confidence Through Faith

The most important ingredient to greater transparency is in your mind. It requires that you build confidence not only in who you are but in what you believe.

Real transparency will come easier if you are not distracted by the things that might happen (fear) and not swayed by the things you think you deserve (pride). Instead, you are willing to live in the truth of what is real and to be comfortable with the result of that reality. That's what it means to live by faith, because faith allows for the acceptance of truth, and truth always produces the best long-term results. Faith allows us to deal with personal insecurities and liberates us to look outside ourselves for lasting solutions to the storms within.

The simple definition of faith is "a strong belief or trust in someone or something." When you think about it, the definitions of pride and fear include those same components. All three words are rooted in what we believe or trust about how life is going to play out for us and who or what is in control of our lives. They are rooted in our truth.

Jon Gordon, the popular author and motivational speaker, points out that the one thing faith and fear have in common is their focus on the future.

"They both believe in a future that hasn't happened yet," he says. "Fear believes in a negative future. Faith believes in a positive future. The antidote to fear is faith, and it's only a thought away."

Pride, meanwhile, sees that future from an inward perspective. It's something you control—it involves vanity and arrogance—whereas faith frees you to look outward so you can do your part and release the results.

Faith in what? In other words, what do you look to for the certainty that destroys pride, defeats fears, and provides confidence in the face of challenges?

Well, it can be a host of things, depending on the situation. For many people, including me, it involves a higher power. I made no critical decisions at Prologis without seeking wisdom from that higher being.

Personally, I believe that if transparency is to become a hallmark of your leadership, then your faith and your beliefs will hold up under the pressure of the world only if they are based on something bigger than yourself. Something you can rely on. Something you believe is able to absorb the toughest things in your life. But a clear mindset also requires an understanding of who you

MY NON-NEGOTIABLES ARE EMBODIED IN THREE PERSONAL TRAITS. IN ALL I DO, I WANT TO BE:

1
a person of excellence

2
a person of integrity

3
a person who is accountable

are and what you stand for. That will inform the non-negotiables in every decision you make.

Have you thought about what they are for you? My non-negotiables are embodied in three personal traits. In all I do, I want to be (1.) a person of excellence, (2.) a person of integrity, and (3.) a person who is accountable. I landed on those three aspirational traits several years ago while preparing for a speech, and since then they have provided me with my ultimate litmus test for decisions. I have them written down, and I refer to them frequently. They provide the backbone of my faith in all I do. In fact, I believe all leaders should develop their own personal compass that can provide them with clarity and transparency in their thoughts and actions.

When I think back to the most pivotal moments in my career, most were times when I had to draw on my knowledge of who I was and my personal compass to move forward with transparency. And the process that supported that transparency—measurement, mentorship, and mindset—provided the foundation that got me through it.

THE DILEMMA REVISITED

We all live and work in environments where there's an expectation that every voice can and should be heard, but ailing cultures will always have people who fight against those expectations. Such was the case when I faced my "dilemma" at Prologis.

You remember the "dilemma," right? The one where I felt pressured to support our CEO's desire to acquire a company for a price that many of us on the management team felt was 50 percent—or $250 million—too high? We were living out a scenario in which the voices of the team were ignored, and the fears, insecurities, and pride of our CEO and his team—including me— were fully on display. Now let me tell you how the best practices I've laid out in this chapter helped me embrace transparency, face my fears and pride, and deal with that dilemma.

The process actually started years before the decision. I was fortunate in that I had been tested, evaluated, coached, parented, mentored, and given ample opportunity to develop a baseline to know the person I was. So as the dilemma unfolded, I already knew that doing what I believed to be the right thing trumped any form of loyalty. That's not always the case for everyone, but it was for me. I also knew it wasn't in my nature to just stay quiet and go along to get along. I had to do something. It's who I was. It's what everyone who gave me some form of feedback expected from me...nothing less.

I also sought advice from as many trusted sources as possible. A former business coach became incredibly important as a mentor to me during this strained time of my life. I knew I could rely on him because of the considerable time we'd spend together. And he not only knew me well, he also knew many of the executives I worked with. During one conversation, he told me the best organizations are the ones that get the "employee experience" right. If that's done correctly, he said, other things like the customer experience fall in place. That hit me like a lead balloon. We were wasting time worrying about the politics of a financial decision when our employee experience was mired in a deep, dark pit. And it wasn't going to get better unless someone challenged the status quo.

I also spent a considerable amount of time in personal reflection, getting up at the crack of dawn to read and meditate. Adversity often creates the opportunity to dig deep to find clarity—to discover or rediscover the truth in which you can place your faith. And I find that clarity comes to me through intentional silence while seeking wisdom with humility in the presence of a higher being.

Finally, I ran my decision through the litmus test of my personal compass. In my view, I can't be a person of integrity without leading with transparency. Indeed, I think that's true for all leaders. In this case, my commitment to integrity pushed me toward transparency while dealing with the dilemma.

As the president of the company, I held a seat on the board. As such, I had a fiduciary duty to vote as a representative of our shareholders. I had to be transparent with my views of what I believed was right in order to properly serve that duty, no matter what the cost. So, I decided to tell our CEO that I did not have his back on this one. In addition, I organized a conference call with our lead director. I included key members of our management team on the call, and we informed him of our views in advance of the meeting. Importantly, I also sought his counsel on how to handle the situation. I tried to be transparent with everyone, even though I knew it could have tumultuous consequences. Ultimately, it did.

The board meeting was the hardest I ever attended. The board spent more than two hours beating up the acquisition. They were well-prepared for the discussion, because they knew the management team disagreed with our CEO on its merits. Finally, an overwhelming majority voted to allow us to buy the company under one condition: that our chief investment officer and I renegotiate the price for $250 million less!

After the meeting, our CEO berated the entire management team for our lack of support. I knew we had done the right thing, but it didn't feel like it. Ultimately, we negotiated a substantial price reduction within the range of the board's directive and bought the company. Of course, the way the situation unfolded made us all look bad, and my already eroding relationship with our CEO became irreparable.

Several months later, in early 2008, I retired from the company. I knew I no longer could work in an organization of shadows, where trust and transparency were as absent as light in a black hole. The culture had become inconsistent with my values, and I no longer felt I was in a position to influence it for the better.

I realize now that my response to the dilemma cost me a job I loved, but it allowed me to live without regrets. I had been sucked into a dark culture, and I was trapped there by my fears of failure and of losing a prestigious position. But I found that transparently stepping out in faith defeated those fears, destroyed that pride, and positioned me for much more success down the road.

Ten months later, that same board called and asked me to return, this time as CEO of a fledgling company. It was an opportunity that would expose a whole new set of fears and all-new challenges to my pride—fears and pride I could only deal with through certainty, faith, and transparency. And as I dealt with my pride and fears, I was in a position to focus on another key aspect of developing transparency in my leadership microclimate: building a 3H-Core.

CHAPTER RECAP

The second step in building your microclimate is to embrace transparency. Increasingly we live in a world of glass houses—an open-access, high-speed world where those looking in demand more transparency from leaders. To become a more transparent leader, you first must become more transparent with yourself so you can better understand who you are and what you stand for.

TRANSFLUENCE IN ACTION

+ Developing an understanding of who you are and what you stand for requires that you:

1. Measure who you are and what others think of you, thereby creating a baseline of self-awareness.

2. Seek mentors who can provide a personal gut check throughout your journey.

3. Establish a clear mindset supported by non-negotiables that inform the decisions you make.

9.

 # BUILDING A 3H-CORE

NO MAN CAN PURCHASE HIS VIRTUE TOO DEAR, FOR IT IS THE ONLY THING WHOSE VALUE MUST EVER INCREASE WITH THE PRICE IT HAS COST US.
– CHARLES CALEB COLTON[64]

When I returned to Prologis, I quickly realized I needed an outlet to talk to another leader who had been battered by the market. Call it mutual commiseration.

We did a great deal of business at the time with Morgan Stanley, so one of our bankers there arranged for me to visit with their CEO, John Mack. I was excited about the possibility. Mack had a stellar reputation as a leader in a tough industry, and he was no stranger to challenges. Plus, we had taken similar paths to the CEO chair, so I felt like we could relate to each other's experiences.

Mack started with Morgan Stanley in 1972, worked his way up the corporate ladder, and was COO by 1997 when the company merged with Dean Witter & Co. Phil Purcell, the Dean Witter CEO, became the CEO of the merged companies. Mack worked for Purcell a few years, then left in 2001. He returned as CEO four years later, taking over at a time when the company was struggling.

Robert Kidder, the lead director for the Morgan Stanley board, said Mack, "effectively stabilized the firm and reenergized our culture."[65] I would reverse that and say that one of the ways he stabilized the firm was by reenergizing the culture. That's the approach advocated by Curt Coffman and Kathie Sorensen, authors of *Culture Eats Strategy for Lunch*. They argue that a good culture is a competitive advantage because it produces financial strength.[66] I agree. So, I was curious as to how Mack had brought that idea to life at Morgan Stanley,

A GOOD CULTURE IS A COMPETITIVE ADVANTAGE BECAUSE IT PRODUCES FINANCIAL STRENGTH.

and I was especially interested in his insights on ground he had covered that I had yet to plow.

By the time we met, Mack already had shown remarkable leadership strength when dealing with the burdens of the financial crisis. For instance, he was under tremendous pressure to sell the company to a competitor. In fact, both the US Treasury Secretary and the head of the Federal Reserve Bank were recommending that he sell. But Mack was convinced that selling wasn't in the best interest of shareholders or employees, so he found other ways to weather the storms he and the company faced.

Imagine his life in 2008 when we spent about an hour on the phone as I peppered him with questions like:

How are you dealing with this mess?

How do you act around your people?

What do you say to them when you know your company might not be around next year?

His sixty minutes of counsel was invaluable in the days, months, and years to come. The thing that stood out the most from our conversation, however, wasn't a policy or a program or a business strategy or the specific words he used with his teams. It was his commitment to who he was as a leader and how he would lead others.

"Walt, I try to manage the company by always keeping in mind what I call the 3H's," he said.

"What are those?" I asked.

"Humility, honesty, and humor," he said.

The most respected leaders, he told me, are those who can manage others with great humility and brutal honesty, no matter how uncomfortable or challenging the situations. And in this day and age, he added, we need a healthy sense of humor, or else we take ourselves too seriously and lose the human aspect of our jobs.

What a simple and wonderful approach! I thought.

To me, what Mack was describing was transparency of a deeper sort. It wasn't just about understanding himself and putting faith ahead of his fears, it was about transparently opening up a window into his soul for all to view. You see, when people saw John Mack, they could see a transparent core set of values—values that set into motion the way he conducted business, the way he treated others, and the way he led. Providing this window into his soul through his values was an even more powerful form of transparency and one he would parlay into success.

I really liked the concepts, but I also was impressed that he'd been so intentional about creating and living an unpretentious approach to leadership. So, I immediately starting thinking about those values and how to apply them in our work at Prologis. I realized pretty quickly that humility and honesty were perfect fits for who I wanted to be as a leader. But I changed the word "humor" to something I felt was broader...something that spoke to why humor was important in the first place...something more about the human aspect of leading...something that spoke to how you treat others. That word was "heart."

I have nothing against humor. I love a good joke or a funny story. Humor in a leader can help make a tough situation feel lighter and not so oppressive. But I realized when I am humble and honest, I don't take myself too seriously, and my natural humor comes out. When I'm not humble and honest, my sense of humor goes AWOL, or it comes across as forced and awkward. I also realized using "heart" added something critical about my view of leadership—an emphasis on seeing the innate value of another person. The heart is a powerful metaphor for a deep, sincere sense of caring for other people. To

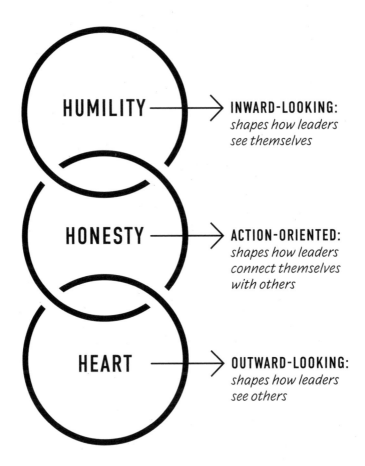

 HUMILITY ⟶ **INWARD-LOOKING:** *shapes how leaders see themselves*

HONESTY ⟶ **ACTION-ORIENTED:** *shapes how leaders connect themselves with others*

HEART ⟶ **OUTWARD-LOOKING:** *shapes how leaders see others*

lead with heart is to love and respect the people around you, not for what they do but for who they are: people, just like you and me.

So, I tweaked John Mack's 3Hs to form what I refer to as my 3H-Core: humility, honesty, and heart.

These values work in harmony with each other and form three interlocking links in a chain that provide strength for the storms of life. Humility is the most inward-looking of the three. It shapes how leaders see themselves. Heart is the most outward-looking. It's about humanness. It shapes how leaders see others. And honesty is the most action-oriented. It shapes how leaders connect themselves with others. In other words, it's the transaction that connects the two together.

They are independent virtues that you live out simultaneously. You might lean into one more than another during certain situations. But if you're ever missing any of the three, you invite trouble into your leadership. On the other hand, when you master them, the other important values fall more naturally into place.

These three values are what I hope people see when I transparently open a window into my soul, and I believe they provide a stabilizing aspect to any leader's microclimate that will equip them for a life of transfluence.

These three values have been expressed and lived through the years by some of the world's greatest leaders. During the Revolutionary War, for instance, John Adams wrote, "I know of no policy, God is my witness, but this—Piety, Humanity and Honesty are the best Policy."[67] Piety, of course, is a commitment to standards that come from something bigger than yourself, so it's a reflection of humility. And humanity is synonymous with heart.

Abraham Lincoln might not have tied the three together, but he spoke of each at different times. One of my favorite Lincoln quotes is about honesty: "I am not bound to win, but I am bound to be true. I am not bound to succeed, but I am bound to live up to what light I have."[68] And he spoke of humility when he said, "I have been driven many times upon my knees by an overwhelming conviction that I had nowhere else to go."[69]

You also hear these themes in the words of former basketball coach John Wooden. For instance, he spoke about the importance of humility and heart when he said, "Consider the rights of others before your own feelings, and the feelings of others before your own rights."[70]

I don't think it's a stretch to say all the leaders I admire most—those I've known personally and those I've studied—reflect these three core values. But I didn't just learn them from leaders in business, sports, and history. The more I thought about them, the more I realized they were rooted in my upbringing. My mom and dad never went to college, but they were incredibly principled, hardworking, and loving parents. Mom worked on an assembly line, picking vitamins for General Nutrition Centers (GNC). Dad had returned home to Pittsburgh from the army in the 1950s with hopes of attending electrician's school, but then his father passed away. So, Dad took over the family grocery store in the crime-heavy Hill District when he was only twenty-three. He ran it until the mid-1960s when he experienced one too many robberies—including the one I mentioned earlier that cost him an eye. (His fake eye became a prop around Halloween, which should give you an idea of his sense of humor.)

My two sisters and I grew up in a middle-class neighborhood. I was young when Dad sold the store and went to work for Kmart, where he was an assistant manager until he retired. Dad, who also was a longtime usher at Pirates and Steelers games, never earned a big salary, but we never lacked for the things we really needed—the really important things like love, discipline, and wise counsel.

The values my parents modeled helped shape me into the man I've become. I haven't always lived those values very well. But, thankfully, they soaked into me enough that something good usually comes out when I am squeezed by the pressures of life.

I could make you a long list of the values my parents taught me—authenticity, dependability, gratitude, respect, truthfulness. They're all important. But if you embrace a 3H-Core, you will be all of these things. Ultimately, I've found other values either flow out of a 3H-Core or support it. They don't replace it.

A 3H-Core is essential for leading in modern climates because these characteristics translate across all cultures and regions. They provide authenticity to the direction and purpose of leadership. They provide the keys to believability and credibility, which are essential elements in our transparent, diverse, and fast-moving world. And they allow leaders to earn trust and thereby have a transformative influence on others regardless of the climates around them.

THE NEED FOR VALUES

Leaders throughout history have a remarkably poor track record when it comes to managing the power that comes with influence. That's because the power that comes with influence feeds our temptations and strengthens our lusts for all sorts of selfish desires—greed, control, sex, status, more power. And in today's world, those temptations are magnified like never before by technology, the speed of global business, and the pressures to keep up with the competition.

Society can be quick to expose, judge, and convict leaders for their shortcomings these days, but how well are these leaders actually prepared to battle the temptations that come with their power? Not very well, I'm afraid.

More importantly, *how well are you prepared?* Not just with policies, procedures, and platitudes about what's right, but with meaningful, deeply held values that ground you as you make challenging decisions during your leadership storms?

Leaders today face the same temptations as leaders throughout history. We must decide if we will be driven by the temptations that come with power, influence, and success, or if we will build within ourselves the types of virtues that honor, serve, and protect others.

I believe this begins with a strong core—an inner microclimate of humility, honesty, and heart.

THE CORE IMPACT

The next three chapters look more closely at each value in the 3H-Core, but allow me to whet your appetite with some examples of leaders who have made them a part of their leadership microclimate.

I think of *humility* when I reflect on the leadership of Lubna Olayan, a rare female CEO in a multimillion-dollar Saudi Arabian-based business. Olayan went to work for her father's business in 1983, and it would be eighteen years before she had a female coworker. By then, she had taken over as CEO of Olayan Financing, and she began quietly working to change that part of their culture.

"I was privileged to be a woman CEO of a large family business," she told *Fortune* magazine in 2015. "I recognized there is something wrong with this—I can't be the only woman."[71]

Olayan has used a soft-spoken style and a business-savvy mindset to champion diversity. That's not easy in a region with a deeply rooted culture that fights against it. But the company now employs around four hundred Saudi women, including more than fifty in their corporate headquarters. The business, meanwhile, has thrived, with revenues, according to sources outside the company, of more than $7 billion a year.

Olayan, however, doesn't label herself as a pioneer or seek publicity for her accomplishments in growing the business or in promoting diversity. She's quick to point out that she's promoting diversity "for deserving people," and she's careful to respect the deeply held traditions of her culture. And in the 150-page networking directory that has photos and biographies of all their managers, her entry falls on page 80 because that's where it comes in alphabetical order.

Rafael Reif, the president of MIT, who sits on a board with Olayan, described Olayan as a unique leader who can quietly drive a conversation without dominating it. Her ability to understand the needs of individuals and the big picture is "an asset and a gift that few people have," Reif told *Fortune*. "Lubna reminds me of nobody."

That explains why Olayan said she prefers "influence" over "power" to describe what she's earning with her leadership. "The more challenges you face in life," she said, "the more of life you experience—this lived experience gives one the 'influence' to impact others' lives."

Humility shapes how she sees herself. She realizes leading an organization isn't about herself, it is about others.

I see *heart* in leaders like Tony Fernandes, the outspoken CEO of AirAsia.

Fernandes is perhaps best known for his leadership in the days and weeks after AirAsia 8501 crashed in late December 2014. Unlike many executives when their organization faces a crisis, Fernandes led from the front with a clear emphasis on caring for the people involved. He proactively communicated with the families of victims and the rest of the world, apologizing for the loss of life, taking responsibility, expressing sympathy. He not only was active in the media, but he met personally with the families within hours of the news about the crash.

In the aftermath of the accident, aviation analyst Mohshin Aziz told the Associated Press that, "The human factor is definitely very genuine, from the words (Fernandes) chooses to the facial expression."[72]

Caroline Sapriel, managing director of the risk and crisis management company CS&A, praised Fernandes for projecting compassion and credibility.

"He is looking after the priorities—the families," Sapriel said. "He is showing a lot of empathy. He is using many channels to put that across."[73]

Fernandes also has been outspoken in his native country of Malaysia and in the region of Southeast Asia when it comes to people-focused reforms.

"Throughout Southeast Asia, politics has been the overriding force while economics and people have come second," he told CNBC. "I think it's prevalent in not just Malaysia, but a few countries. As a businessman, I hope politicians go back to managing the economy, putting people first, and dealing with the politics later."[74]

Heart shaped how he sees others. He understood the inherent value of people, and that understanding influenced his actions.

And I see *honesty* in leaders like Joe Torre, the former manager of the New York Yankees.

Torre had a mediocre career as a manager with the Mets, Braves, and Cardinals, so Yankee fans were less than thrilled when he was hired to lead their team in 1996. But he lasted twelve seasons in arguably the toughest managerial job in baseball, making it to the post-season all twelve years, winning six American League pennants and four World Series titles.

The New York sports market is, and has always been, driven by access, diversity, and acceleration. It has a diverse fan base and players who come from all over the world. The city moves so fast it never sleeps (as Frank Sinatra put it). And the media—which no longer just includes radio, television, and newspapers—is ever-present and never lacking for opinions. Torre understood the pressures of these climates, so he embraced a management-by-trust style with the Yankees. Honesty was a cornerstone element.

"Even now I may have trouble when I have to tell someone the truth if it's not a pleasant thing, but I won't lie to them," Torre said in *The Yankee Years*, a book he co-wrote with Tom Verducci. "I can't do that. The only way you can get commitment is through trust, and you've got to try to earn that trust."[75]

Torre developed a reputation among the hard-charging reporters and columnists in New York for being informative without compromising his team, a trait that was appreciated as much by his players as by the press.

"My one point to the players was they were never going to read something that they haven't heard from me, at least something significant," he said in *The Yankee Years*. "And that's part of the trust I try to create."[76]

Honesty shaped how he connected himself with others. He understood his actions shaped how others saw him as a leader and how they responded to his leadership.

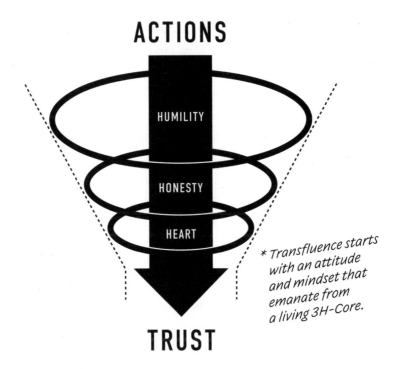

ACTIONS

HUMILITY

HONESTY

HEART

Transfluence starts with an attitude and mindset that emanate from a living 3H-Core.

TRUST

FROM VALUES TO INFLUENCE

Leaders like Olayan, Fernandes, and Torre found success because they developed a leadership microclimate marked by strong core values. A 3H-Core helps leaders navigate what to share, when to share it, and how to share it—all of which are key to building trust. In fact, when you look at people, processes, and programs that aren't building trust, they usually are missing one or more of these core values. Likewise, if you filter decisions, policies, programs, and other actions through a 3H-Core, you'll set them up for success.

Transfluence starts with an attitude and mindset that emanate from living a 3H-Core. A strong 3H-Core motivates transformation in ways that are more meaningful, more noble. You can move people to action with coercion, incentives, or inspiration. They don't require a 3H-Core. Coercion is pretty universally seen as a weak approach to leadership. It's still widely practiced, of course, but it's fragile and hard to maintain. Incentives and inspiration have their place, but their results aren't sustainable if they aren't built on trust. Without trust, people soon see the incentives as gimmicks and the inspiring speeches become phony and hollow. But when you open a window into your soul, you bring humility, honesty, and heart into your leadership patterns for everyone to see and experience. That creates a microclimate that's sincere and worthy of trust. And as you'll see, it's a microclimate that's transformative.

CHAPTER RECAP

The third step in building your microclimate is to build a 3H-Core of humility, honesty, and heart. A 3H-Core is transparency of a deeper sort. It's not just about self-awareness, mentoring, and mindset, it's about having a core set of values and opening up a window into your soul for all to see. When you lead with humility, honesty, and heart, you put yourself in a strong position to earn trust, especially in this fast-paced world where people are clamoring for believability, credibility, and authenticity.

TRANSFLUENCE IN ACTION

+ Be humble in the way you see yourself as a leader.

+ Treat others with a heart that shows them they matter.

+ Display honesty as you live out who you are and how you connect with those around you.

PART IV: LIVING IN YOUR MICROCLIMATE

TRUST MEN, AND THEY WILL BE TRUE TO YOU;
TREAT THEM GREATLY, AND THEY WILL SHOW
THEMSELVES GREAT.
– RALPH WALDO EMERSON[77]

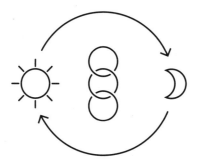

LIVING MY 3H-CORE
IS A DAILY DECISION TO
CONSISTENTLY ACT ON
HUMILITY, HONESTY, AND HEART.

Imagine for a minute that you are a frog sitting on a log in your favorite microclimate—a pond. It's a warm, sunny day, and you're just hanging out with four of your frog friends. As the day heats up, three of you decide to jump into the water for a swim.

So how many frogs now are on the log?

It's a trick question, of course, one often used to make a point by consultants with clients and parents with their children. The obvious but wrong answer is two. The actual answer is five, because there's a difference between deciding to do something and actually doing it. We can decide to lose weight, run a marathon, or jump in a pond, but nothing really changes until we actually act on those decisions.

The same is true of our values. For me, living my 3H-Core is a daily decision to consistently act on humility, honesty, and heart. Acting on those values strengthens my microclimate, which helps me continue to act on them in the future. A closer look at each element of the 3H-Core can help you understand these values better, act on them more consistently, and strengthen your microclimate. Otherwise, you might spend all day just sitting on a log.

GUIDEPOST NO. 6

HUMILITY PUTS OUR PRIDE AT RISK.

RISK IT ANYWAY.

10.

HUMILITY: DON'T TRUST US, WATCH US

FOR EVERYONE WHO EXALTS HIMSELF WILL BE HUMBLED, AND HE WHO HUMBLES HIMSELF WILL BE EXALTED.
– JESUS OF NAZARETH[78]

John Wooden, the legendary basketball coach at UCLA, once accepted an award for outstanding leadership from the Kravis Leadership Institute at Claremont McKenna College.

The sixty-acre campus just south of Los Angeles is home to one of the best liberal arts schools in the country. Its alumni include the governor of Montana (Steve Bullock) and prominent business leaders like Michael Jeffries (former CEO of Abercrombie & Fitch), Robert Nakasone (former president and CEO of Toys R Us), and Peter Thum (founder of Ethos Water and a former vice president of Starbucks). The late actor/comedian Robin Williams studied political science at Claremont, although he didn't graduate from the college.

When it comes to sports, however, Claremont McKenna doesn't draw the top athletes or command the attention of rabid fans. With an enrollment of around 1,200 students, its athletic teams compete in the NCAA's Division III level. The school doesn't provide athletic scholarships, so sports are truly extra-curricular activities that students participate in for the love of the game.

In short, the environment couldn't be more different from the high-profile campus of UCLA, where Wooden led teams loaded with future NBA stars to ten Division I national titles during the final twelve years of his Hall of Fame coaching career. But Wooden seemed right at home at Claremont when he showed up for the awards banquet. In fact, Ronald Riggio, the professor with the honor of

"THE MAIN INGREDIENT OF STARDOM IS THE REST OF THE TEAM."

JOHN WOODEN

presenting the award, was struck by the uncommon ease and sincerity Wooden displayed while interacting with students during dinner. Riggio saw firsthand why Wooden had such a stellar reputation as a leader—why so many leaders quote him, study his famed "Pyramid of Success," and try to emulate his approach.

Wooden had enough great quotes on selfless leadership to fill a book. My favorite? "The main ingredient of stardom is the rest of the team."[79] Those sorts of quotes can be educational and inspiring, but Riggio experienced something even better: he got to see how Wooden actually *personified* some of the quotes that he had made famous.

"Just before his after-dinner speech, Coach Wooden turned to me and said, 'I think if I had it to do all over again, I would coach Division III,'" Riggio recalled in a blog for *Psychology Today*. "I was stunned. Here was the greatest coach in the history of NCAA Division I sports, saying that he would give away all of the glory and attention for the 'love of the game.' ... Coach Wooden displayed his sincerity and his humility. Coaching was not about him, but about the student athletes and the success of their shared endeavor."[80]

Riggio's conclusion: "The very best leaders are confident but display great humility."[81]

I couldn't agree more. That's why humility is part of a 3H-Core in my leadership microclimate. Humility shapes how leaders see themselves. Humble leaders have the courage to face their fears and set aside their pride. They are believable and credible because they share credit and take responsibility for their actions. People look at them and see a microclimate that includes selflessness, even within a larger climate that tempts them to shine light on themselves. Unfortunately, humility is a quality that's hard to come by and even harder to keep in a world of glass houses.

THE BLAME GAME

You could argue that arrogance found in attitudes and behaviors at every level of an organization is merely an expression of our changing cultural norms. That's just the way it is in our "Big Me" world. So, you could blame arrogance on social media, television, movies, video games, parents, teachers, politicians, and the like.

The point is, it's easy to blame anyone and everyone but ourselves for the arrogance around us. But if we want to end organizational arrogance, we have to start with ourselves. As I said earlier, humility is about how we see ourselves. How we see ourselves shapes how others will see us. And how others see us drives how they respond to our leadership.

Wooden saw himself as a basketball coach who could make a positive difference in the lives of his players. He didn't see himself as the king of a basketball dynasty or as the CEO of a factory that churned out NBA talent. His humility helped him earn trust and succeed as a leader on and off the basketball court.

Humility, as Wooden exemplified and as great thinkers throughout time have said, is critical to a well-lived life. The English cleric Charles Colton called humility the "constant companion" of truth.[82] The poet Thomas Moore said it's "that low, sweet root from which all heavenly virtues shoot."[83] Author Thomas Merton said it's what "makes us real."[84] Philosopher Simone Weil said, "Real genius is nothing else but the supernatural virtue of humility in the domain of thought."[85] And Albert Einstein said, "A true genius admits that he or she knows nothing."[86]

Ralph Marston, a Texas-based author known for his short, motivational blogs, points out that humility first and foremost benefits the person who is humble. When times are tough, he says, it allows you to "step back from taking the troubles personally" and "seek and accept advice and assistance." When times are good, it "shields you from dangerous delusions of grandeur" so you can "generously extend the benefits of your success far beyond yourself."[87]

As New York Times columnist David Brooks points out, humility is also almost always a core trait in the people who earn our respect and trust.

"All the people I've ever deeply admired are profoundly honest about their own weaknesses," Brooks writes. "They have identified their core sin, whether it is selfishness, the desperate need for approval, cowardice, hardheartedness or whatever. They have traced how that core sin leads to the behavior that makes them feel ashamed. They have achieved a profound humility, which has best been defined as an intense self-awareness from a position of other-centeredness."[88]

Moreover, I've yet to find any research that doesn't confirm the value of humility to the bottom line of business. The nonprofit Catalyst, for instance, released a study in 2014 on inclusive leadership that surveyed 1,500 workers in six countries—Australia, China, Germany, India, Mexico, and the US. The overriding implication, the authors of the study said, is that "to promote inclusion and reap its rewards, leaders should embrace a selfless leadership style."[89] Acts of humility such as "learning from criticism and admitting mistakes," they said, are key traits in inclusive leaders. And, in fact, researchers have found that embracing what's known as "intellectual humility" is vital to a leader's learning development. In short, when we embrace the fact that we don't know everything, we become more proactive about pursing knowledge and more willing to collaborate with others.

I experienced this firsthand when I began working on my MBA at Harvard. During the first day of my first class, the instructor opened the discussion for comments about a case study that we had been assigned to read in advance. The hands of roughly seventy of the ninety students in my class shot into the air. Each student who was called upon weighed in with what seemed to me to be a thoughtful interpretation of the case. I was stunned and, quite frankly, a bit fearful to give my interpretation. My hand never went up, and I kept my mouth shut. I went back to my room a little deflated. Two humbling thoughts dawned on me: 1.) I was going to school with a bunch of barracudas! 2.) I was determined to keep up and learn from my peers. If I hadn't embraced intellectual humility, I'm not sure I would have survived.

SEEKING HUMILITY

In a world that honors adulation and self-promotion, humility is easy to admire but hard to master. So how do we master it?

The good news is, we don't have to give up our ambitions or check our business acumen at the door to lead with humility. We also don't have to deny the talent and skills we bring to the table that help make our organizations better.

Humility isn't a *show of weakness* in a leader; it's a *show of meekness* in a leader. I'm not talking about the spineless type of meekness many people think of when they hear that word. I'm talking about *meek* as it's defined in the original Greek—a word that describes a wild animal, like a horse, that has been tamed. It's the picture of a strong animal that's learned to control itself so it can use its strength in positive rather than destructive ways.

Humble leaders aren't weak; they accept that they have weaknesses, and they exercise control of their strengths. Humble leaders aren't passive; they are willing to recognize when they are wrong and take corrective actions. And humble leaders aren't unassertive; they let their actions speak louder than their words. A humble leader still looks people in the eye...still offers a firm grip on a handshake...still makes tough decisions that won't please everyone. In fact, humility requires confidence, courage, and tremendous strength—all qualities that build trust.

To incorporate humility into our leadership microclimate, we have to take a deep inward look at ourselves and then consistently do at least three things: 1.) Ask. 2.) Listen, and 3.) Be accountable. All revolve around one key concept that you've probably picked up on by now: taking the focus off yourself. Rick Warren, author of the mega-bestseller *The Purpose Driven Life*, offered a straightforward definition of humility that drives home this point: "Humility is not thinking less of yourself; it's thinking of yourself less."[90]

Asking and Listening. We live and work in world that seems to spin in hyperdrive, and often that leaves little time for asking questions and listening to what others have to say. After all, we have places to go, people to see, and things to do. And, as Christine Porath, an associate professor at Georgetown's McDonough School of Business, points out, the access to ideas, information, and opportunities through technology only makes us busier.

"It's increasingly challenging to be present and to listen," Porath said in an essay for *The New York Times*. "It's tempting to fire off texts and emails during meetings; to surf the Internet while on conference calls or in classes; and, for some, to play games rather than tune in."[91]

But asking and listening from a place of humility opens the doors to a multitude of benefits—from self-improvement as a leader, to better customer service, to stronger relationships with employees, to powerful solutions to business challenges.

I talked about this some when I shared Frank Blake's commitment to the inverted pyramid style of management. Blake learned to look outside of himself by putting himself at the bottom of the pyramid, which meant he had to work hard to communicate up to those who were doing the bulk of the work by asking the right questions and aggressively listening to answers.

David Alexander, the former president and CEO of TruGreen, also has experienced the fruits of asking and listening. David, who retired from the Memphis-based lawn care company in 2018, told me that "quality and honesty" in communication are vital to building trust. David visited sixty to seventy of the company's 260 locations each year just to spend time listening to associates and asking them questions. At the home office, he had a monthly luncheon with twelve employees from different departments to hear what they were thinking. And he knew approximately six-hundred employees by name, including all 250 who were at the manager level. (He used flashcards, by the way, to help with memorization.)

It's amazing to me how powerful it is to address someone by their name when they might not expect it. I remember working hard to memorize employees' names when I was an executive at Prologis. It was hard and took time, and often it was overwhelming, but I'm confident it paid off in greater trust. It takes intentional effort and is even more effective if you spend time with people to get to know them so you can connect the details of their lives with their names and faces.

Alexander's approach to leadership was particularly important because he took over for a CEO who had come to TruGreen with some hard-and-fast ideas about how things needed to be run and, therefore, developed a reputation for actively not listening to the opinions of others.

"For about eighteen months," Alexander told me, "they made a number of decisions around pricing, around systems, and around customer service even though the whole field leadership team was constantly saying there were reasons those decisions might not be good for us."

On the surface, some of the decisions regarding services for customers and operating systems for the company made perfect sense. In practice, however, they didn't produce the intended results. TruGreen went from adding about 900,000 new customers a year to adding just 600,000 in 2012. Service levels—the percent of time they showed up on the day they should have—dropped from 90 percent to 60 percent. And TruGreen's financial performance took a dive.

Alexander spent his first six months visiting branches, asking questions, and listening to answers. During the second half of that year, he began implementing changes based on recommendations from frontline leaders. Among other things, the company used employee surveys to help define their core values, they switched to a new operating system that better fit the business, and they began offering tiered lawn care services that ensured quality while still giving customers a range of options.

"By the end of the year," Alexander said, "there was a tremendous amount of trust created through that."

By 2014, the company once again was profitable, was handing out millions in bonuses, and was seeing its name on local and national lists of the best places to work. In 2018, when Alexander retired, the company had annual sales of around $1.4 billion, up from around $980 million in 2012.

Alexander's humility allowed him to ask the right questions and genuinely listen to the answers. Then he acted in ways that were best for the company. But leading with *humility*, as David leads, isn't always the same as *being humble*. I know of a former CEO of a large organization who was considered "humble" by some who knew him—a genuine person who wasn't full of himself. But he didn't always demonstrate humility as a leader because he seldom interacted with his workforce. He ate lunch in his office, never in the employee cafeteria. He had a private parking garage separate from where other employees parked. And when he walked through their stores, he was surrounded by security guards and unable to connect with his employees. He may have been humble to some who knew him well, but his actions didn't show it. He wasn't *demonstrating* humility because he wasn't transparent enough to make himself available, much less to ask employees questions and listen to their answers.

Humble leaders also ask and listen to their customers.

Paul English, CTO and co-founder of the corporate travel site Lola.com, has been known to put this principle into action in several ways, including by literally answering to his customers. When he was running Kayak, the travel search engine he co-founded and later sold to Priceline.com, English put a red telephone with a loud ringer in the middle of their office in Boston. When customers called the help number on Kayak's website, it rang to that phone, and English often was the guy who answered it.

"I love talking to customers, even angry ones," English said at the time. "I learn a lot from them about how to make the site easier to use. When the call's over, I'll say, 'If you have any follow-up questions, my name is Paul English; I'm the co-founder of the company.' I'll give out my personal cell-phone number. Only one out of 20 people might actually call, but they're blown away when I do that."[92]

Humble leaders also eagerly expose themselves to constructive personal feedback.

There's a scene in the 1988 movie *Beaches* when Bette Midler's character is dominating a conversation. After a lengthy, self-absorbed monologue, she says, "But enough about me. Let's talk about you. What do you think of me?" She, of course, was asking out of pride, searching for adulation, hungry for ego biscuits.

Humble leaders ask the same question, of themselves and of others, but with different motives. They are willing to open a window to their souls and admit they don't have all the answers. They ask themselves the tough questions, and they allow others to ask them tough questions. They listen with an open mind. And they are strong enough to face their personal fears and insecurities, so that they can grow into better leaders.

Be Accountable. When we're accountable to our values, our emotions take a backseat and courage gets behind the wheel. When we're accountable to the various congregations around us, it's our selfishness that takes a backseat, and the greater good gets behind the wheel.

Harry S. Truman often referred to what eventually became a very famous sign on his desk in the White House. It said, "The buck stops here." It was, and is, a great reminder to take responsibility and not "pass the buck" to someone else. But it's important to remember that Truman took responsibility because he felt a *sense of responsibility.*

Truman was president of the United States of America—some might say the most powerful person in the world. Yet, he felt a deep sense of accountability to others. He didn't pass the buck, but he never thought he *owned* the buck. Like all US presidents, he answered to the Constitution, to the other branches of government, and, ultimately, to the citizens across the country. Truman didn't say, "The buck stops here" because he was all-powerful and all-knowing, but because he was a leader who felt the enormous weight of a humbling responsibility. He was humble enough to be accountable.

When I was CEO of Prologis, I often felt humbled by the obligation of answering to our employees, our board, our investors, our customers, and our business partners. Others reported to me and answered to me, but I answered to everyone. I felt responsible, and, therefore, accountable.

It's not enough, however, to know we are accountable. We have to *be accountable* to others. People have to see accountability in our actions. For me, that included standing in front of people who held me accountable, hat-in-hand, without posturing, blaming others, or deflecting criticism. When I returned to Prologis, the first thing I did was make sure the management team embraced humility in ways that were visible to everyone connected to our organization.

First, we needed to be open and honest with each other about our mistakes and put the past where it belonged—behind us. We would learn from it, but we wouldn't live in it, and we certainly wouldn't repeat it. This, by no means, was easy. We had to model it, insist that others hold us accountable to it, and vigilantly hold ourselves accountable to it.

Next, we needed to demonstrate humility to our people. We openly shared our mistakes with them in our first town hall meeting, and we committed to creating a culture of openness, good news or bad news, as we moved forward. Then we continued to openly communicate updates, even when things weren't going as well as we wanted.

Finally, we had to show humility to our investors and stakeholders. More than a thousand of them were listening to us at a meeting in New York when we opened our presentation with a laundry list of our mistakes. We basically told them we'd done a lousy job managing the company prior to the recession, and it was our goal that it would never happen again.

"Don't trust us," we told them. "Watch us."

In other words, we let them know their trust was something we had to earn over time with our actions. And we eventually did earn it. It was a vulnerable moment for us, but it laid the groundwork for building trust in the future.

In business, leaders tend to take credit when things are going well. When things go poorly? It's the economy or the market or some other uncontrollable factor that got in the way of leadership's brilliant policies and strategies.

Organizational arrogance stems from arrogant leaders, but humble leaders are believable and credible because they don't fear taking responsibility for their actions. The slippery slope to lost trust often begins when a leader puts himself or herself on a pedestal and, intentionally or unintentionally, stops answering to others. Humble leaders take an inward look at themselves as servants whose job is to be accountable to others. That accountability drives humble leaders to win trust and, in doing so, accomplish great things.

A LESSON IN HUMILITY

Life is a masterful teacher. And, personally, I've found humility is one of its recurring lessons—perhaps the best lesson anyone could have.

One of my most memorable lessons in humility came during the first few years after I graduated from college. I had a degree in accounting, a job with a prestigious accounting firm, and a girlfriend who for some unknown reason would never see how perfect her life would be if she simply hitched her wagon to my rising star. I proposed to her three times during the seven years we dated. *Three times*. And she politely rejected all three offers.

I might not have been Harrison Ford or Tom Cruise, but I didn't think I was terribly hard on the eyes. I had done well academically at a respected university. I had a good job making a better-than-average salary. And I had a promising future. What wasn't there to like?

Turns out, I was what you might have called a *great investment*: someone you would want to buy for what I was worth and sell for what I thought I was worth. But her repeated "no thank yous" felt like three big, fat rejections of my self-worth. Strike one. Strike two. Strike three. You're out. Thanks for playing the game of love.

Talk about lessons in humility!

In retrospect, of course, we weren't a good fit. She was a terrific person, and we enjoyed spending time together, but we didn't share the same passions or the same hopes for the future. It actually was appropriate that we never married, but it was hard to understand at the time because my ego was in control. As time went on, I realized her rejections saved us both some heartache. That lesson in humility stuck with me as I moved forward in life. And as my life unfolded, of course, I met Sue and discovered someone who was a perfect match for me.

Throughout my life, in personal and professional situations, I've had to set my pride aside and humbly deal with reality. It's been the only way for me to make good decisions that moved me and those I served forward in a positive, productive way.

As leaders, when we remove the facade of pride and add humility to our core, we unleash a powerful force for establishing transfluence. It changes our mindset, and it establishes a foundation for trust and influence.

CHAPTER RECAP

People look at humble leaders and see a microclimate that includes selflessness, even within a climate that tempts them to shine light on themselves. When you remove the facade of pride and add humility to your core, you unleash a powerful force for establishing transfluence. Remember, humility isn't a show of weakness in a leader. Instead, humble leaders accept that they have weaknesses, and they exercise control of their strengths. They recognize when they are wrong, take corrective actions, and let their actions speak louder than their words.

TRANSFLUENCE IN ACTION

+ Consistently do these three things to practice humility as a leader:

   1. Ask

   2. Listen

   3. Be accountable

GUIDEPOST NO. 7

HONESTY OFTEN LEADS TO CONFLICT.

NEVER WAIVER FROM THE BATTLE.

11.

HONESTY: LIVING THE POLICY

HONESTY IS THE FIRST CHAPTER IN THE BOOK OF WISDOM.
– THOMAS JEFFERSON[93]

Look across the landscape of corporate value statements, and you'll see it dotted with some form of the word *honesty*.

For instance, twelve companies appeared on *Forbes'* list of "best companies to work for" each of its first eighteen years, and seven of them publicly listed their "values." Five of the seven use the word *honesty* or a related word like *trustworthy* or *integrity*. Even the companies that don't expressly list it as a "value" give indications that it's central to their business philosophy. Wegmans talks about caring, respect, and empowerment—all ideals that are impossible to live without honesty. Publix says it is, "dedicated to the dignity, value and employment security" of its associates. Dignity is a fruit of honesty's vine.

Let's face it: most companies publicly say they're committed to some form of honesty, even if they're lying through their teeth when they say it. Enron's values, for instance, included "integrity." And in the wake of its price-gouging scandal, Turing Pharmaceuticals put a fifteen-page "Global Code of Business Conduct" on its website that said it expected employees to "act with good faith and integrity."

The only business I can think of that ever openly touted its dishonesty was the fictional organization KAOS. As all *Get Smart* fans remember, KAOS regularly referred to itself as an international organization of evil. With departments like the League of Impostors and the Contrived Accident Division, dishonesty was a core value for KAOS.

Real organizations, of course, aren't so open about their dishonesty, and neither are the leaders who set their standards. But no matter what's listed on

IT DOESN'T MATTER WHAT YOU SAY YOU BELIEVE, IT ONLY MATTERS WHAT YOU DO.

their values statements, there is one test for determining if honesty *really* is a part of a leader's core vocabulary: actions. As Robert Fulghum noted in *All I Really Need to Know I Learned in Kindergarten*, "It doesn't matter what you say you believe, it only matters what you do." You can't just preach honesty; you must "live" honesty. You might rise partly on your charisma and charm, but you will fall when you're consistently exposed as dishonest.

There are exceptions, of course, but I'm convinced that dishonesty ultimately is a cannon ball shot into the hull of trust, and it quickly sinks a leader's credibility. You see, while humility is how leaders see themselves, and heart is how they see others, honesty is the active transaction that connects the two. Without it, a leader has nothing.

AN HONEST DISCONNECTION

Most people, perhaps even politicians, value honesty and see themselves as honest. The Barrett Values Centre, which uses an assessment tool to measure and map the values that impact an organization's culture, has found that honesty ranks the highest among the personal values employees consider most important.[94]

Leaders are no exception. Ask them if they value honesty, and they'll say they do. Ask them if they lead with honesty, and they'll say that they do. And if you gave them some sort of "honesty challenge" that required them to decide between an honest or dishonest behavior, they'd probably score rather well. But dive into their daily actions, and, well, you might find their honesty has limits.

That's because the path to dishonesty begins on a slippery slope filled with good intentions. The real world is complicated, and we're seldom met only with large black-or-white dilemmas—*should I embezzle millions or should I not?* Instead, we're met with a series of small dilemmas, all colored in various shades of gray. We can start to see minor indiscretions as justifiable because we see the bigger picture and convince ourselves that a small lie or an omission of a few facts will serve the greater good. Intentions that start out pure end up polluted by a slow and sometimes minor but constant dripping of dishonesty.

In the aftermath of the Volkswagen emissions scandal, then Chairman Hans Dieter Pötsch blamed the crisis in part on "a mind-set in some areas of the company that tolerated breaches of the rules" that arose from pressure to improve sales in US markets.[95] I wonder if something similar happened with Theranos, the once red-hot health care company with a mission "to make actionable information accessible to everyone at the time it matters."[96] Sounds great, right? The plan was to build devices that cheaply and accurately performed dozens of tests on a single drop of blood. Among other things, this could help patients with early detection and prevention of diseases. And what could be nobler than using technology to improve our collective health and well-being?

The Barrett Values Centre has found that honesty ranks the highest among the personal values employees consider most important.

HONESTY
COMMITMENT RESPECT
ACCOUNTABILITY POSITIVE ATTITUDE
FAMILY HUMOR/FUN INTEGRITY
COOPERATION BALANCE (HOME/WORK)

The problem arose when the accuracy of the tests fell into question. Owning your own data about your health isn't so great if the data isn't accurate. In March 2016, the Centers for Medicare and Medicaid Services released a 121-page report listing all types of deficiencies in the Theranos lab in Newark, California. By July 2016, regulators had revoked the company's license to operate the California lab and banned founder Elizabeth Holmes from working in the blood-testing business for two years.

And things would only get worse. In March 2018, the Securities and Exchange Commission charged Holmes and former company president Ramesh Balwani with fraud. The SEC said Holmes and Balwani raised "more than $700 million from investors through an elaborate, years-long fraud in which they exaggerated or made false statements about the company's technology, business, and financial performance."[97]

Holmes resolved those charges against her, in part by giving up control of the company and reducing her equity in it. That June, a federal grand jury indicted her and Balwani on charges of wire fraud. Both pleaded not guilty. Then in early September 2018, the new leadership at Theranos sent an email to investors announcing the company had shut down. It began releasing its assets and cash to creditors, but equity investments in the company, according to *The Wall Street Journal*, were made worthless.

Investigative reports have painted an ugly picture of the Theranos culture, and generally traced the ugliness directly back to Holmes. It became clear that her deceptions of others—and her self-deceptions—created a culture where questions and doubts were seen as personal attacks against her and, therefore, not tolerated. This created an incredible pressure to live up to the delusional hype, and the company as a whole lacked the honesty needed to admit mistakes, build trust, and deliver on its claims. As a result, a microclimate of dishonesty developed throughout the organization, and trouble followed.

HONESTY ISN'T A PRETZEL

There are appropriate times, of course, to withhold information. When I advocate for honesty as a core component of a leader's microclimate, I'm not talking about sharing everything we know. That's impractical, illogical, and, in some cases, counterproductive.

Some leaders, however, withhold or twist information for the wrong reasons. They lie for self-protection. They manipulate information to serve their personal agenda. Maybe they aren't comfortable giving up control, or they don't trust people to deal with reality, especially if a situation is fluid. Ultimately, they haven't dealt with their fears. Even if their intentions are honorable, their insecurities and pride prevent them from the type of transparency that builds deep trust and creates positive influence.

I've come to discover that there's more to honesty than "not lying." In far too many cases, leaders use that low-bar standard to avoid demonstrating real transparency. The fact is, many leaders can be honest but not trustworthy because of what they *don't say or don't do*. It reminds me of a friend who was a somewhat rebellious teenager. He came home one night intoxicated, and his mother confronted him.

"Have you been drinking beer?" she asked.

"No, I haven't," he told her.

In fact, he had been drinking whiskey. So, he didn't lie. But was he speaking honestly? Of course not. He was the furthest thing from transparent with his mother.

Likewise, some leaders avoid real honesty by carefully constructing their words like a lawyer crafting an agreement full of loopholes. They communicate the things they like and avoid the topics that are uncomfortable. They create a perception of full disclosure that holds water about as well as a sieve.

Some leaders also keep people under-informed about reality, good or bad, and thus invite people to speculate about what's going on. Before long, their false perceptions become reality. No information becomes misinformation, which spreads like a wildfire—inside the company and across the internet. And misinformation weakens trust.

I experienced this in a personal way shortly after I was named CFO of Prologis. At the time, we had acquired a refrigerated logistics business that was separate from our real estate warehouse business. This company moved frozen goods throughout the US for customers like Kroger, Albertsons, and Kraft Foods. From the beginning, the business had all sorts of operational issues that led to negative financial results. So, while it only represented about 10 percent of our overall business, it accounted for about 90 percent of our headaches.

Our real estate investors never understood our decision to enter this business and continually criticized us for doing so. We desperately wanted to prove them wrong—and ourselves right. When we reported poor results to Wall Street, we tended to focus on issues that seemed like one-time problems—the bad weather in France that affected the pea harvest, for instance. We didn't want to add fuel to their "I told you so" fire. At times, I found myself in a position where I felt we weren't completely leveling with the Street.

The business continued to underperform—every single quarter—and we began losing credibility. In the end, our investors had a right to be concerned. We found out the hard way and ultimately sold the business at a loss of more than $100 million.

That was a real lesson to me about coming to grips with the truth immediately, even when it's tough. As the old saying goes, a real leader faces the music, even when he doesn't like the tune. We never lied. But we could have been more open and forthright...with our investors and with ourselves. We emphasized the facts that didn't matter and de-emphasized the facts that did matter. It was a black eye that we could have avoided if we'd acted more forthrightly from the beginning.

Because access to information (and misinformation) is so easily available and spreads so quickly—and because a diverse workforce makes for fertile ground for growing misconceptions—the need for honesty in leadership has never been greater. In fact, leaders can't just *be honest*, they must *make their honesty known*. We live in a world where perceptions are reality, and people tend to hear only those messages that support what they already think. The battle against confirmation bias is often a battle to align perceptions with truth. The hard work of making truth known is why consistent, effective communication is so vital to leadership. It's almost impossible for leaders to over-communicate an important message—you can't say it too often or find too many different ways to share it.

When lived out well, a commitment to honesty and to making your honesty known will shape perceptions in ways that strengthen culture and our brand as a leader. Our honesty becomes the binding force in our personal connections with others. It's an expression of our humility and our heart. It's no longer just about truthfulness; it's about being truthful in humble, respectful ways. It's goes beyond the surface level and creates a connection that strengthens the trust and respect we need to be influential. It allows us to influence others because they believe us and believe in us, not because they fear us or because they are obligated to us. It replaces the forced influence of positional authority with the *transfluence* of relational authority.

But this type of honesty involves sharing our thoughts, opinions, and feelings, admitting to the world that we don't have all the answers, and opening ourselves up to constructive criticism. We end up exposing ourselves to potential wounds. We become vulnerable to attack, both from the enemies around us and the demons within us.

What does it take to consistently lead with this type of honesty? It takes the courage to act boldly and an emphasis on morals over medals.

HONESTY TAKES COURAGE

People crave and respond to honesty that's driven by courage.

It requires leaders to be honest with themselves and others. It requires leaders to take positions that are unpopular. It requires leaders to share things that create discomfort—for themselves and for the people around them. And it requires leaders to act in a timely fashion, because procrastination erodes trust.

I've found, for instance, that sometimes you have to "share the math" even if you haven't solved all the equations. By that, I mean a leader needs to go into details that might be uncomfortable or even unclear to help people understand a situation and buy into the direction they're taking.

Like me, my friend, Debra Cafaro, led a company through the financial crisis. And during that time, she discovered how honesty—when backed with actions—alleviates fears and builds trust.

"During the financial crisis," she told me, "anyone who wasn't scared was insane, because everyone was on the abyss—the whole world."

Cafaro is the chairman and CEO of Ventas, a real estate investment trust that owns around 1,200 health care-related properties in North America and the UK. Since she took over in 1999, the company's market capitalization has grown from $200 million to more than $21 billion in early 2020, and she's been recognized as one of the "world's 100 most powerful women" (*Forbes*) and a "top 50 best-performing CEO in the world" (*Harvard Business Review*). In 2009, however, when things were at their worst, she remembers openly telling people that the "world was on the abyss" but that she was going to do everything in her power to protect the company and its people.

Those words were nice, but she followed them with a bold, honest, and straightforward action plan that was different from what they had followed in the past. For instance, she directed her teams to take an about-face on growth.

"We had to really just completely reverse everything we had been doing and thinking," she said. "I remember telling them to stop buying and start selling. For me, it was being able to outline actions that would make the company stronger and make people feel like we were doing something, because action can be an antidote for anxiety."

We faced a similar challenge in 2008 as we worked to stabilize the financial health of Prologis, and one thing quickly became clear: we were going to have to lay off a large chunk of our workforce. We were built for rapid growth throughout the world, but the markets were telling us the world would see very little growth in the years ahead. Our leadership team analyzed the numbers and debated what we needed to do. Some thought we should cut 10–15 percent of our workforce, but others felt that the number should be much greater. Depending on how long the recession would last, either path could have been right. Ultimately, we believed the recession would be deep, so we agreed the right number was 25–30 percent.

Now, one out of every three to four people is a huge reduction for any large company, and we had never gone through massive cuts in our history. We weren't just cutting out some fat in the organization; we were cutting into a lot of bone. I kept wondering how we should handle it. What should we do to make sure we treated people with dignity? How could we ensure the people who left felt fairly treated and those who stayed still had respect for their employer? I also wondered about the best timing. It would take us around forty-five days to figure out which people we would let go. How and when should we tell people what was happening? As you can imagine, there were a lot of rumors swirling around the company, and unaddressed rumors turn into reality in the minds of people. On the other hand, how could we provide answers we simply didn't have?

The easy option was to say nothing until we had all of the facts to answer everyone's questions. But sometimes honesty isn't about what you do, it's about how people perceive what you do. It may require that you deal with the elephant in the room when people want or expect you to deal with it, not when it's necessarily the best time for you. We realized people wanted to hear what we were thinking, even if our plans weren't solidified. They wanted us to explain the math, even if they didn't fully understand it, show them our thought process, even if it was incomplete, and reveal our struggles so they could understand what it was like to be in our chairs. They wanted to be in it with us. They wanted to help. And our authenticity with them counted.

After making an announcement, we immediately held a company-wide town hall meeting, and Bill Sullivan, our CFO, walked them through the math. We told them we had to make cuts, or we would severely risk everyone's future. We told them the magnitude of those cuts even before we had an implementation plan with specific names and departments. And we committed to treating everyone with dignity and consistency. In short, we told them what we knew before we knew everything. By doing so, we risked losing good people prematurely, and we knew it might not be good for morale. But we felt transparency through brutal honesty was more important in the long run.

And do you know what happened? Our people embraced the situation. They processed what they heard and were sympathetic to our decision. Of course, they were worried about their jobs, but they would have worried anyway. Opening up with them gave everyone time to think through what was going to happen and why. That was critical, because pain is always better after we have time to process it.

To this day, I can't think of many people, if any, who were unhappy about the way they were treated. Many thought they should have been chosen to stay, but, in general, we received very high marks for how we handled the situation. And some of those employees came back to work for the company when times improved. Most importantly, the workforce that remained saw how we handled adversity—with the courage to be brutally honest—and we gained the respect we needed to tackle bigger things that were soon to come.

HONESTY VALUES MORALS OVER MEDALS

Sir Philip Craven, the president of the International Paralympic Committee, pulled no punches when he announced that no Russian athletes would be allowed to compete in the 2016 Paralympics in Rio.

"Their medals over morals mentality disgusts me," Craven said of the Russian government.[98]

If you followed the Olympic Games in 2016, you know Russia was at the center of one of the biggest controversies because investigators found wide-ranging evidence of corruption in the country's anti-doping system. The International Olympic Committee decided to let each individual sport's governing body decide which Russian athletes could compete, but the Paralympics committee took a more sweeping stand by allowing no Russians to participate. Craven said the Russian government had "catastrophically failed its para-athletes" with the "complete corruption of the anti-doping system."[99]

"Their thirst for glory at all costs has severely damaged the integrity and image of all sports," he added, "and has certainly resulted in a devastating outcome for the Russian Paralympic Committee and para-athletes."[100]

Many things in life are good until they are abused. In this case, it appears the Russians took positive things like national pride and a competitive spirit and corrupted them because they valued medals over morals—they allowed pride to trump truth. This resulted in dishonesty that tainted the victory of every Russian athlete competing internationally, and, in some regards, all athletes. The Guardian said the anti-doping controversy "overshadowed the buildup to the Rio Olympics" because of accusations that the IOC's lack of action was "further eroding trust in sport and potentially leaving viewers unable to believe what they are watching."[101]

I'm as competitive as anyone. I enjoy winning—on the golf course, in a game of cards, and in the world of business. But the taste of victory can't be savored when it's laced with the bitterness of dishonesty. And while dishonesty might produce some short-term results, it almost always gets exposed—even more so nowadays because technology enables the watchdogs and gives them greater voice. When dishonesty is exposed, trust is the first victim.

You might ask if honesty actually pays off in business. Does it lead to things like higher profits and more market share? Well, not always...at least not in the short run. The Russians likely would have won a lot of medals at the Paralympics if their dishonest practices hadn't been exposed, and each medal won dishonestly would have come at the expense of those who competed within the rules.

Or consider the world of competitive golf, where Blayne Barber missed out on an entire year on the PGA Tour because he realized he had signed an incorrect scorecard. One of the ways up-and-coming players earn the right to play on the PGA Tour is by finishing at or near the top in tour qualifying tournaments. In 2012, it looked like Barber had earned his tour card in one of those tournaments, even though he had assessed himself a one-stroke penalty for brushing a leaf with his swing on a bunker shot. Later, however, he learned the correct penalty was two strokes. He could have kept quiet about his mistake, but he self-reported the error, even though he knew the result would be more than another stroke added to his score. That's because the error meant he had signed an incorrect scorecard, and the penalty for that is disqualification from the tournament. For Barber, that meant another year in the minor leagues of golf.

Those types of stories happen every day in business. Dishonest leaders often win, costing honest leaders what they earned. And honest leaders miss out on rewards because they self-report their mistakes, even when no one else would have known. Honesty simply offers no guarantees of financial profit or worldly success.

That said, we live in a society that rewards what it views as noble behavior. Companies who prove themselves as honest and ethical often see spikes in customer loyalty and positive word-of-mouth marketing that strengthens a brand and drives future sales. Beautycounter, for instance, publishes a "Never List" of more than 1,500 chemicals and ingredients it won't use in its products out of concern for consumer safety. The ingredients are legal and, in many cases, less expensive than the alternatives. But CEO Gregg Renfrew is committed to honesty about what goes in their products and the impact those ingredients might have on the consumer. So, she doesn't hide the ingredient list or justify using cheaper, more harmful ingredients. And guess what— Beautycounter has built a fiercely loyal customer base as a result.

Patagonia provides another example of the value of morals over medals. The clothing company is famously driven by its commitment to the environment. So, it focuses on making quality, durable products that last longer and, therefore, don't need to be replaced as often. The company once ran an ad that said, "Don't Buy This Jacket" as part of its effort to convince consumers not to buy more things than they need. And they share their planet-friendly R&D results with competitors. Most clothing companies, of course, want you to replace what you wear long before it wears out. They want you to buy ten jackets—one in every color. And they never share intellectual property.

Patagonia shows that honesty isn't just about telling the truth; it's also about being open with information that helps others. If everyone wins, then the company's higher purpose wins. Their honesty is driven by their values and not their bottom line. It's hard to say what it really costs them in long-term sales or growth, but it's easy to see the benefits to their profitability. From 2008, when CEO Rose Marcario joined the company as its CFO, to 2015, profits more than tripled. Patagonia had a 14 percent growth rate during those years. Patagonia's founder Yvon Chouinard told *Fortune* that, "Rose understands business better than I ever did, and she understands the need for revolution. She's the one who's going to lead us there."[102]

Patagonia's transparent practices have prompted a lot of talk about leading by example. Marcario is quick to say while they're not the size of Nike, they can still do their best to make it uncomfortable for other businesses not to follow them. Patagonia clearly sets a high values bar for its marketplace and earns points for courage in the process.

Ultimately, of course, honesty is a personal value. It's a personal choice, one we have to make at every decision point we face. But the impact of our honesty—the impact of those choices—cascades throughout our organizations and beyond. If we're not personally living this value that we all agree is critical, the culture will follow our lead. But if we live it daily, in the little things as well as the big things, we'll build the type of trust that stands the tests of time.

CHAPTER RECAP

Plenty of leaders claim to be honest. In fact, you'd be hard-pressed to find someone in a leadership position who doesn't make that claim. But there is one test for determining if honesty really is a part of your leadership microclimate: actions. Your actions will have a measurable impact on the level of trust you create. And those actions need to consider the perceptions of the people around you. You can be honest but not trustworthy because of what you don't say or don't do or how you carefully construct words like a lawyer crafting an agreement. Real honesty takes courage. It can be tough to tell people things they may not want to hear. It may require you to deal with a situation before you are ready. And sometimes it may mean you need to deal with the elephant in the room, even if that's uncomfortable.

TRANSFLUENCE IN ACTION

+ These four simple actions can help enhance the perceptions others have of your honesty as a leader:

1. Avoid procrastination on matters you know someone is expecting you to deal with. Addressing expectations in a timely fashion wins trust.

2. Consistently communicate over and over and over again and in multiple ways. People often hear what they want to hear and not necessarily what you say, so a simple, consistent message helps align perceptions with reality.

3. Be aware of what your silence is saying and manage it appropriately. There are times when silence is required, but silence often gives false perceptions room to take root and grow.

4. Don't allow pride to trump truth, and always convey the truth, even if it's the most painful thing you can do.

GUIDEPOST NO. 8

LEADING WITH HEART REQUIRES TRUST.

GIVE TRUST A CHANCE.

12.

HEART: LESSONS FROM THE GARBAGE TRUCK

HOW FAR YOU GO IN LIFE DEPENDS ON YOUR BEING TENDER WITH THE YOUNG, COMPASSIONATE WITH THE AGED, SYMPATHETIC WITH THE STRIVING AND TOLERANT OF THE WEAK AND STRONG. BECAUSE SOMEDAY IN YOUR LIFE YOU WILL HAVE BEEN ALL OF THESE.
– GEORGE WASHINGTON CARVER[103]

I took a work-hard, play-hard approach to my college years at Penn State. I put in the hours it took to make good grades, and I usually had a job, sometimes two, to help pay my way. But I also teetered on the edge of irresponsibility from time to time.

Sometimes I fell off that edge. Once I was actually thrown off.

It happened the summer I came home from college thinking that I might take a bit of a break from work. My dad had other ideas.

"Get a job," he said.

"Where?" I asked.

"Put on your suit," he told me, "and we'll go find something."

First, we went to the steel mills, and I put in a few applications. They all told me they didn't have any openings, but they'd get back to me. Then we went to the city's sanitation department—Dad heard they might be hiring garbage men for the summer. They looked me over and also said, "No." And so it went.

That afternoon, after a tiring day of rejection by the city's manual-labor industries, I decided to unwind at a party with some fraternity brothers from college. The unwinding involved a few kegs of beer, which allowed me to toast my failed job hunt with my buddies. They laughed at the thought of me showing up at the steel mills and sanitation department in a suit. And the toasting, laughing, and unwinding continued until I found my way home and passed out on the couch around 3 a.m.

I woke up thirty minutes later with a ringing in my ears. It was the phone.

"This is Pete from sanitation," the voice on the other end said. "I need you to come in."

"Jerry, don't do this to me," I said. "I need to get to sleep."

Gerry Sacunas was one of my fraternity buddies, and I assumed he was the prankster making the call.

"No, no, no," said the voice. "This is *Pete*. At the sanitation department."

I hung up the phone and searched through bleary eyes for the number I had gotten during my interview. When I found it, I punched the numbers into our phone.

"Hello, this is Pete," said the man who answered. "You're hired. I need you to be at work in an hour."

Reluctantly, I got off the couch and reported to work. The supervisor looked me over suspiciously and asked the obvious: "Are you drunk?"

"Yes, sir," I said.

"Can you do the job?" he asked.

"Yes, sir," I said.

He shrugged, pointed me toward a truck, and off I went with one of the crews.

You know how celebrities often go by just one name? *Cher...Bono...Sting... Madonna...Pitbull....* Well, this crew was sort of like that. I got first names or last names, but never both. Jimmy drove, and Patterson and I rode outside, standing on a ledge and hanging onto a handle. We went into neighborhoods and worked our way from house to house. Patterson and I would hop off at each home, empty the cans of trash into the back of our truck, and hop back on to go to the next house. We didn't go very fast, except when we were between neighborhoods. Then the truck might hit speeds of up to fifty miles an hour.

"You OK," Patterson said during one such stretch.

I wasn't looking too good or feeling too good, but I nodded that I was fine. Then we rounded a curve, and the truth was revealed in dramatic fashion. I lost my grip, flew off the truck, and landed thirty feet later with a thud in someone's front yard. It was painful, but I survived. Once Patterson and Jimmy determined I wasn't dead, they laughed hysterically.

It didn't take long for that story to become like folklore among all the other garbage men. I can't say that was the proudest moment of my life, but it somehow endeared me to the other members of the team for the entire summer. I had unwittingly earned some credibility in their eyes. Those guys became my best pals. I wasn't like them in many ways, but they took me under their wing for that summer. I can still say that picking up garbage was one of the coolest jobs I've ever had.

These guys were real people. They were a bunch of good guys doing unglamorous work to make a living for their families. And the experience of working with them that summer stuck with me as a reminder that everyone you lead is human. They have friends. They have families. They have hobbies. They have dreams for their future. They experience joy. They experience pain. They make mistakes. And they do great things.

Working on that garbage truck reinforced an important lesson my parents modeled for me while I was growing up: there's a basic level of respect we should give to everyone—a respect for their humanity. This is why "heart" is a core value in the microclimate of transfluence.

While humility is about how we see ourselves, our heart shapes how we see people and how people see us.

When they see us, do they see leaders who are human? Leaders who are vulnerable? Leaders who share in their struggles? Or do they see leaders who are condescending? Leaders who view themselves as above or better than those they lead? The great football coach Vince Lombardi once said, "to be a leader, you must be honest with yourself and know, as a leader, you are like everyone else, only more so."[104] No matter how big our salary or the size of our office, we all make mistakes, we all have troubles, we all want to experience joy, and we all have needs. When we lead with heart, we open a window into our souls and allow others to see us as we truly are—as human.

The flip side is that our heart also shapes how we see others. Are they just another "asset"? Are they an "expense"? A "number"? Or do we see them as something more? Do we see them as souls—flesh and bones with a mind, body, and spirit—not just in the way we think about them but in the way we treat them? How we see people drives how we treat them. When we respect people for who they are, not just what they do, we naturally treat them with kindness, compassion, and empathy.

HOW WE SEE PEOPLE
DRIVES HOW WE TREAT THEM.

My friend, David Alexander, told me a story that I think is a great example of how a leader can live this out. When he became CEO of TruGreen, one of the things David did was create core values for the company based in part on input from his employees. They collectively decided that a core value would be the Golden Rule—to treat others the way we would like to be treated—and that they would live it out in five key areas: service, teamwork, community, safety, and integrity. They made efforts to emphasize this value and the importance of living it out in all five key areas, but the most dramatic statement came in a decision David made that he never expected to become public knowledge.

A few months after rolling out the program, one of the company's drivers was involved in an accident in Michigan. There were no serious injuries, but the other vehicle was totally destroyed by a TruGreen truck. Since Michigan is a no-fault state, the company wasn't liable for the accident, but the man who lost his car called David and asked for a favor.

"I have no car," he said, "and I have no insurance and I have a child with cancer that I have to take in every week for treatment. I realize you're not liable, but would TruGreen be willing to rent a car for me?"

David got off the phone, called the company's general counsel, and arranged to buy the man another car—not because he was legally obligated, but because that's how he felt he should live out the Golden Rule in this situation. Word leaked out, of course, and as more decisions like that became known, his employees realized they would be supported for doing the right thing.

It's probably clear by now that I'm a fan of John Wooden, and Wooden would say that this type of heart-led approach to leadership comes from a healthy view of your value as a person. When he was growing up, his father would tell him, "Remember this, you're as good as anybody. But never forget you're no better than anybody, either."[105]

Wooden modeled that in many ways. For instance, at the 1972 Final Four in Los Angeles, Wooden, whose teams had won seven of the previous eight national titles, waited in a long line for more than an hour with all the other coaches to register and pay his $20 dues for annual coaches' convention. And at the 1974 Final Four in Greensboro, North Carolina, Wooden saw a group of high school coaches eating breakfast and asked if he could join them. So, on the morning that his team would play in the semifinals of the NCAA Tournament, Wooden chatted causally for about ninety minutes with these coaches about basketball, life, religion, and anything else that came up. Finally, one of them suggested that he might have something better to do than spend time with them. Wooden just smiled and said, "I can't think of anything I'd rather do."[106]

THE HEART OF A CAREGIVER

Wilt Chamberlain was one of the greatest basketball players of all time. When he was traded to the Los Angeles Lakers in the late 1960s, he was asked if he thought his new coach could "handle" him.

"No one handles me," Chamberlain reportedly said. "I'm a person, not a thing. You handle things. You work with people."[107]

Intellectually, I think most leaders know people aren't tools to control. They aren't a "thing" to be handled or a "chair" that merely fulfills a function. But it's easy to grow detached and distant from the very people who matter most in our organizations. It's easy for leaders, even those of not-for-profits, to become "caretakers" of their organizations rather than "caregivers" for their organizations. It's easy for them to get fixated on net worth rather than human worth.

We were under a tremendous amount of pressure as a leadership team when we were trying to turn things around at Prologis, and much of our focus was on our financials. We were working dog years, and the tension among us was building. I could see that if the torrid pace continued, we'd soon all be dead. An intervention was clearly needed. So, I decided to hire a coach to work with the entire senior management team, one-on-one and as a group. And in one of our first meetings, he told me something that has stuck with me ever since.

"The best-led teams always understand and actually behave as though human capital is their most valuable asset," he said. "Is your team doing that?"

Actually, I didn't know. I had heard leaders say that. Many even put it in their value statements. But how many just pay lip service to it? How many really mean it? What does it mean to place human capital first? And how does it look to actually place human worth before net worth?

That's when I realized our senior management had fallen into a common leadership trap—we led with a "caretaker" mentality. We did what I think most leadership teams do: We took care of the company. We focused on areas for growth. We paid attention to new acquisitions. Our performance assessments always started with our financial results. We talked about our customers and how we could improve our share of their wallet. And we made sure we communicated to our investors.

All of those things are important, but I realized we rarely talked about our people outside the context of their performance and compensation. We didn't talk about ways to enhance their experience. We rarely even talked about what was important to them. We took good care *of the company*, but we gave less care *to its people*.

We needed to make a shift from that "caretaker" mentality to a "caregiver" mentality—a servant approach toward our people. We needed to lead more with a heart.

I'm on the board of directors of Iron Mountain and Host Hotels, companies that have taken a caregiver approach toward human capital. Their leaders have a fundamental belief that their workforce strategy is a competitive weapon. They devote time in every board meeting to showcasing their people and they place enormous importance on continuous personnel development deep into their organizations. It's an excruciating process, but one that demonstrates their heart for their people. And their track records of employee retention prove their strategy is working.

This is the type of leadership that the modern workforce craves and responds to, because it focuses on human interactions and relationships. It lives and breathes empathy. It speaks to people where they are in life and knows what matters to them. And it demonstrates respect for the unique qualities of diverse employees and other congregations. Transfluent leaders want their people to be better individuals inside and outside of the work environment— with their families, friends, and in their communities. And they engender trust because subordinates know their leaders have their backs.

INVESTING IN HEART

Some people see no place for "heart" and "love" in leadership. They think it's soft and weak. But more and more organizations are discovering the business value of heart. Yum! Brands, owner of Pizza Hut, Taco Bell, and Kentucky Fried Chicken, has put thousands of employees through a "Heartstyles" training. It includes a "character development tool" that measures behaviors related to humility, love, pride, and fear. And *The Wall Street Journal* reported in 2016 that Cisco Systems, Breakthru Beverage Group, and Ford Motor Co. were among the many companies "investing in empathy training to improve management, retain employees, or guide design decisions."[108]

Leadership speaker JP Pawliw-Fry has a unique way of demonstrating how we truly value emotional qualities of leaders over technical or intellectual qualities. I was in the audience one day when Pawliw-Fry divided the room into two groups. He gave us all three sticky notes to write on. He asked half of the room to write down the three most exceptional characteristics of the best leader they had ever worked for, one characteristic per sticky note. The other half of the room wrote down the three most challenging characteristics of the worst leader they had ever worked for. Again, one characteristic per sticky note. Then he asked each participant to place their sticky notes on one of three easels: one with the header "IQ" for intellectual qualities, one with the header "TQ" for technical qualities, and one with the header "EQ" for emotional qualities (emotional intelligence). In other words, were their best or worst characteristics technical, intellectual, or emotional in nature?

Like other audiences who had done this exercise, we were stunned to see around 95 percent of the sticky notes ended up on the EQ easel. And it didn't matter whether they were good or bad, the characteristics that stood out most were almost all tied to emotional intelligence. Why? Because people trust leaders who care about them, and they despise leaders who don't. We assume leaders will have technical and intellectual qualities. We expect our leaders to be smart. We expect our leaders to have the technical skills they need for their jobs. But it's their relational skills—those that come from their heart—that really shape the quality of their leadership.

When people are promoted in your organization, are they evaluated to see if their emotional skills are suited for their new roles? In most organizations, the answer is no. In fact, most organizations don't test their future leaders at all. Many promote solely on technical skills, intellectual abilities, or tenure. Too often, people are promoted to do something they just aren't capable of doing. Nine times out of ten, it's because they were promoted into leadership roles they weren't prepared to handle. And after the promotion, they aren't counseled in how to succeed. Ultimately, organizational trust suffers.

In caregiving organizations, those that place a high value on leading with heart, coaching and mentoring are front and center in strategic importance. They create awareness in at least five areas for every employee in their organizations.

First, they make sure all employees have a clear understanding of their strengths and weaknesses. An assessment can create a baseline of facts not opinions. There are a number of personalized tests that can be taken in the market. Everyone in every organization should take one, have the results evaluated with them, and have them communicated to appropriate managers in the organization.

Second, they make sure all employees know what others think of their performance. It's surprising to me how many organizations still don't conduct 360-degree evaluations for their entire team. They should. Continuously. (But only with the motive of developing employees.)

Third, they make sure all employees know how to apply the organization's strategy and values in their day to day jobs. This needs to be enforced over and over in discussions and evaluations in superior/subordinate relationships.

Fourth, they make sure all employees are given continual opportunities to improve their skills and value throughout the entire organization.

And finally, they make sure all employees are challenged to live out the organizational values—at work, at home, and in their communities. People need to be encouraged to think broadly about their contribution to society. In doing so, they will make better managers when the time comes for them to do so. I find that in most organizations, rarely does this final discussion take place. It should.

Organizations that place a high value on heart also invest time with their people. I traveled frequently as an executive with Prologis, but I typically spent a few days each week at our headquarters in Denver. When I was there, I rarely had lunch with another member of the senior management team. Instead, I made it a point to pick someone in the cafeteria whom I didn't know well, buy them lunch, and spend a half an hour with them talking about their jobs, families, and concerns. I spent most of my time asking questions and listening.

We also instituted brown bag lunches where I met with whole departments to answer questions about whatever they wanted to talk about. When I traveled to our different offices, I'd sit down with our employees— usually fifteen to twenty—and we'd talk about whatever they wanted to discuss. Sometimes I had answers for them, and sometimes I didn't. The most important thing was that I tried my best to invest time with them. I got to know them and learned what mattered to them, personally and professionally. People respected that, and it helped me earn their trust.

My friend, Debra Cafaro, knows that building trust is a product of spending time with people, but she also knows that some of those interactions don't come with smiley-face emojis. Cafaro, as I mentioned previously, is the chairman and CEO of Ventas, a real estate investment trust that focuses on the health care industry. She's learned that earning trust requires authenticity, and authenticity is sometimes a bit messy. By working through differences in sincere and respectful ways, she's earned trust that creates loyalty and results in value, not divisiveness.

"I still get mad occasionally," she told me. "I lose my temper more than I would like. I have extreme standards for performance and excellence. So, I can mix it up in ways that are not always models of good leadership. But people know I'm being honest. And I tell people this who are new to our organization. Look, I might get mad in the moment. But we end up solving problems and supporting each other no matter what goes wrong."

The disagreements are easier to overcome, she said, if you've invested thousands of interactions that involve positive, constructive praise. People are more likely to speak up with differing views or take risks if they've seen a leader reward those actions over and over and over. And they are more likely to forgive a leader who has proven over time that she genuinely cares. I've learned over the years that spending time with people and getting to know them is the best way to appreciate them for who they are, not just what they do. And when they know you appreciate them for who they are, you build trust.

THE MARK OF HEART

In my efforts to develop a strong microclimate for transfluence, I've found that the core value of heart begins with respecting humanity and then shows up within a leader in three key ways: by trusting others, by serving others, and by recognizing others.

1. Trusting Others. It's hard, if not impossible, for leaders to earn trust when they are unwilling to trust the people around them. That's why the best leaders know how to delegate—and to truly let go of a task or project and let others drive it.

This is hard for many leaders, because successful leaders tend to rise through their organizations by getting things done. They fear (there's that word again) that if they aren't in control of something, it won't get done well enough. So, they do it themselves or they micromanage someone else.

If you can't trust your people, however, you have the wrong people in place. That doesn't mean people must be perfect. You aren't perfect. Why should you expect that of others? When you trust others, you have to accept the reality that they sometimes will let you down. When they fail, will you push them out? Will you second-guess yourself and hold ever-more-tightly to control? Or will you help them up, offer grace, and use it as a teachable moment?

When you don't trust others, they still grow—but they grow frustrated. And then they usually do one of two things: they stay and contribute negative energy to your culture, or they leave for opportunities elsewhere. Either way, you lose.

Elise Mitchell, who built a successful public relations company from scratch and now is CEO of the global PR network owned by communications giant Dentsu Aegis, put it this way in her book *Leading Through the Turn*: "If you don't truly release leaders—if you don't empower, equip, and enable them—you'll discover that the talented, capable, smart people you worked so hard to get on your team will soon leave for some other team. And they should ... Why would anyone stay with somebody who's selfish, driven by power, and hungry for credit?"

2. Serving Others. Leaders with a heart are always servant leaders. The two go together like turkey and dressing. When someone looks into the window of our soul, we want them to see a heart that serves. As rabbi/author Harold Kushner pointed out, that is what life's really all about.

"The purpose of life is not to win," Kushner says. "The purpose of life is to grow and to share. When you come to look back on all that you have done in life, you will get more satisfaction from the pleasure you have brought into other people's lives than you will from the times that you outdid and defeated them."[109]

Serving others, in other words, will warm your heart. But serving others typically takes the form of sacrificing for others. That means we give up some

THE MARK OF HEART

TRUSTING OTHERS:
Release tasks or projects to your team.

SERVING OTHERS:
Take care of the people around you.

RECOGNIZING OTHERS:
Share the glory that comes with victories.

of what we have—fame, power, position, authority—so that they can shine. If we don't value people—if we don't have a heart for others—then we won't sacrifice for them. Think about the person in the world you love the most—you no doubt value that person so much that you would sacrifice anything for his or her well-being. As leaders, we have to care enough about the people around us that we sacrifice for their well-being. And ultimately, their well-being contributes to our well-being, and we win together.

3. Recognizing Others. When we trust others and serve others, we will watch them shine. And if we lead with heart, we will make sure they get due credit for who they are and what they do for the organization. Our modern climates feed the need for recognition and enable it on an unprecedented scale. A leader's responsibility is to appropriately share the glory that comes with victories. Stories of individuals and teams provide not only recognition, but encouragement and inspiration. That's how teams get better.

Wikipedia learned this firsthand. The editors who voluntarily create and update pages on the site are keys to the company's success. So, with the help of UCLA assistant professor Jana Gallus, Wikipedia conducted an experiment by randomly selecting some of the four thousand eligible editors to receive an award. The editors use pseudonyms, which meant there was no real personal gain from the awards, just a digital image on their personal page and recognition on an official Wikipedia page. The mostly symbolic awards, however, increased productivity by 13 percent over eleven months, increased retention by 20 percent, and led many of the editors to take on even more work.[110]

At Prologis, we devoted one-third of our town hall meetings to sharing stories about how people around the world were doing a great job for the company. This was an ongoing initiative, not a one-time thing, and this type of consistent, broad-based recognition is critical for the modern leader. Today's diverse workforce, for instance, creates a reality in which employees often are scattered across the world, some working from home or a coffee shop. And, of course, these employees have vastly different socioeconomic and cultural backgrounds. A narrow approach to recognition ends up shining a light only on a few top performers for the very specific things they achieve and the ways they've achieved those things. A broader approach finds ways not only to honor a variety of people in a variety of roles, but to do so in ways that are most meaningful to them. The rewards and recognition you give a Hindu worker from India might look very different from those you would offer a Muslim worker from Turkey or a Christian worker from Mexico.

CONDUCT YOUR ORCHESTRA

When a leader's microclimate includes heart, that leader, without fail, will operate as a conductor not a soloist.

Soloists perform alone, with little or no help from others, and they crave recognition in the same way a singer on stage covets a standing ovation from the audience. When the spotlight homes in on a soloist, it's all about their personal performance. It's not that they don't need to trust and serve others, or that others don't play a role in their success, but they are living in a very self-focused moment.

Conductors, on the other hand, understand that their success is tied to the success of those around them. They create an environment in which all the performers trust in themselves and each other. They serve everyone in the orchestra to ensure each individual and each section is in a position to work together and bring their music to life. They organize, inspire, empower, and monitor. They win only if everyone wins with them.

Conductors, in short, trust their people, serve their people, and recognize their people. So do great leaders. They lead with heart.

CHAPTER RECAP

There's a basic level of respect you should give to everyone—a respect for their humanity. This is why heart is a core value in the microclimate of transfluence. As a leader, people expect you to be smart and to have the technical skills you need for your job. But it's your relational skills—those that come from your heart—that really shape the quality of your leadership. The best-led teams always understand and actually behave as though human capital is their most valuable asset.

TRANSFLUENCE IN ACTION

+ Make the shift from a caretaker mentality to a caregiver mentality and actively lead by:

1. Trusting others

2. Serving others

3. Recognizing others

To do this, you must lead like a conductor, not a soloist: organize, inspire, empower, monitor, and win with your teams.

GUIDEPOST NO. 9

PURPOSE AND MEANING ARE FLEETING.

NEVER GIVE UP ON THEM.

TWO KEY INTERTWINED MOTIVATORS DRIVE TRANSFLUENT LEADERS— PURPOSE AND PASSION.

We've talked about the difficulties of leading in today's climates and how those challenges can divert us from achieving the single most important aspect of leadership—being transformatively influential, or transfluent, in the lives of those we lead. Transfluent leaders effectively deal with the storms that surround them by looking outside of themselves, embracing transparency, and acting authentically through humility, honesty, and heart. But truly transfluent leaders don't just build a microclimate that governs how they lead. They also use their influence to change the world around them. They don't just thrive within the climates around them. They actually impact and transform those climates.

In other words, transfluent leaders are a force of nature. Two key intertwined motivators drive these leaders—purpose and passion. Let's explore what it means to take transfluence to this higher level by embracing these qualities and becoming a positive force of nature in today's climates.

PART V:
BEING A FORCE OF NATURE

THIS IS THE TRUE JOY IN LIFE, ... BEING USED FOR A PURPOSE RECOGNIZED BY YOURSELF AS A MIGHTY ONE; ... BEING THOROUGHLY WORN OUT BEFORE YOU ARE THROWN ON THE SCRAP HEAP; ... BEING A FORCE OF NATURE INSTEAD OF A FEVERISH SELFISH LITTLE CLOD OF AILMENTS AND GRIEVANCES COMPLAINING THAT THE WORLD WILL NOT DEVOTE ITSELF TO MAKING YOU HAPPY.

– GEORGE BERNARD SHAW[111]

13.

➤ PURPOSE: LESSONS FROM A SECOND-GRADER

WHAT IS THE USE OF LIVING, IF IT BE NOT TO STRIVE FOR NOBLE CAUSES AND TO MAKE THIS MUDDLED WORLD A BETTER PLACE FOR THOSE WHO WILL LIVE IN IT AFTER WE ARE GONE?
– WINSTON CHURCHILL[112]

I don't really know what all I learned as a second-grader at McAnnulty Elementary School in Pittsburgh, but I'll never forget what I learned from a second-grader at Maxwell Elementary in Denver.

A friend and I were visiting the inner-city school as volunteers for Junior Achievement, the nonprofit that helps kids learn about business and develop work-readiness skills. We were there to teach and inspire young students. Frankly, I had no expectation of learning anything from them.

Man was I wrong.

We showed up and gave a talk about the importance of our communities and how certain jobs—police officers, firefighters, and the like—were vital to our survival. After the lesson, we spent time talking more specifically about our jobs. I did my best to keep it simple. I talked about how I was in the real estate business and that we constructed buildings for companies that needed to use them.

When I finished, a little girl tugged at my pant leg and looked up at me with big, brown eyes.

"Sir, if you build things for people," she said in a low and somewhat fearful voice, "can I ask you a favor?"

"Of course," I said. "What would you like?"

"Can you build me and my grandmother a house that we could live in?"

I was stunned, and I had no idea what to say. So, I did what any second-grader would do in that situation: I looked to the teacher for help.

Only about half of the students in this class lived regularly with one or more of their parents, she told me. Roughly a third of the class had at least one parent who had been incarcerated, and many of her students were effectively homeless, living from place to place.

I looked at the little girl and regretfully told her I couldn't build her a house, but that I wanted to help her in other ways if I could. At the time, I just wasn't sure what those ways were.

As we prepared to leave, the teacher stressed the importance of her students having role models in their lives and thanked us over and over for taking time out of our busy schedules to be there. I realized that day that she deserved all the thanks. And I also realized that it would be completely irresponsible of me if I didn't use my sphere of influence to do something about the challenges she and her students faced. So, over the next few years, we began committing our Prologis workforce in Denver to educating kids in the inner city. We worked with Junior Achievement throughout the city and also adopted an elementary school near our corporate headquarters. Our employees taught classes, raised money, sponsored clothing drives, held holiday parties, and conducted career days—all for kids from underprivileged communities.

More than half of our local workforce participated in something. For them, it was a powerful experience. For me, this was transformative influence in action. It was a revelation to see how much our people wanted to give something of value to those who were in need. What was troubling, however, was how little time our employees had in their lives to devote to these types of activities. Understandably, their business worlds and families took up most of their time. Many didn't and, in fact, couldn't make time for this vitally important role in society.

Something needed to change, and it started with how I saw my purpose as a leader and the purpose of our corporate role in society. My experience with the second-grader in that inner-city school in Denver helped raise my awareness about my need, and our company's need, to rally around a higher purpose that creates broader opportunities for extending transfluence. It helped me better interpret my world and the world around me. And over time, I realized providing opportunities for our people to excel, lead, and add value in society wasn't just our *corporate responsibility*—it was our *core responsibility*.

Organizations that don't provide that sort of leadership are out of touch with how best-in-class companies are increasingly run today. More importantly, they're missing a great opportunity to positively influence their world. And when they miss that opportunity, they fail to meet their obligation. Fulfilling this core responsibility only happens when leaders are motivated by a higher purpose—for themselves and for their organizations.

William Pollard, former chairman of ServiceMaster, was known for embracing this core responsibility as a leader long before it became a popular mantra in the business world.

"People want to work for a cause, not just a living," Pollard wrote in *The Soul of the Firm*, which was originally published in 1996. "When there is alignment between the cause of the company and the cause of its people, move over, because there will be extraordinary performance!"

MEANING THROUGH PURPOSE

As human beings, we crave purpose. Ask any pastor, priest, monk, imam, rabbi, politician, philosopher, or psychologist.

Steve Taylor, an author and senior lecturer in psychology at Leeds Beckett University, calls the need for purpose a "defining characteristic" of people. "Human beings crave purpose and suffer serious psychological difficulties when we don't have it," he said. "Purpose is a fundamental component of a fulfilling life."[113]

Many philosophers and psychologists consider meaning through purpose a key to joy and a critical factor in resilience. In fact, Viktor Frankl made it central to his groundbreaking psychological theory known as "logotherapy." In his seminal book *Man's Search for Meaning*, Frankl quotes German philosopher Friedrich Nietzsche as saying, "He who has a 'why' to live for can bear almost any 'how.'" And as a survivor of Nazi concentration camps during the holocaust, Frankl's research and theories were backed by the most extreme forms of personal experience.

When you find meaning in a purpose that's outside of yourself—something outside of the storms of life and the climates that create them—it takes you out of the shadows and into a place where your motives are genuine, and your influence becomes meaningful and truly transformative. It empowers you to admit your mistakes, listen respectfully to others, surrender control, and act with courage and conviction. It tells you that you can fail and still survive, grow, and rebound for new victories. You aren't dependent solely on your own powers or skills or intellect. You aren't defined by the results of any particular moment in time. You have a certainty that's tied to things way beyond what you can control or achieve on your own.

Victor Strecher, a professor at the University of Michigan and the director of Innovation and Social Entrepreneurship, points out that we've known philosophically for centuries that a purpose in life is good for us, so he set out to research the benefits.

"Now there is this amazing science to the philosophy," he says in a video about his book, *Life on Purpose.* "People who have a strong purpose in life live longer, they're less likely to develop heart disease, they're less likely to develop stroke. Ten years later, people with a strong purpose in life are half as likely to develop depression as people with a low purpose."

And if those aren't enough benefits for you, he adds that, "If you have a strong purpose in life, you have better sex. Nice."[114]

Unfortunately, as Strecher also points out, we live in, "an increasingly nihilistic world," where many people don't aspire to "something beyond just watching the Kardashian sisters on television and seeing what they're doing."[115]

What's interesting to me is that our "big me," self-absorbed culture still values purpose in theory, and it's especially relevant among emerging leaders. A study commissioned by McGraw-Hill Education found that 73 percent of graduating students said finding a job that allows them to do what they love was more important than finding a job that pays well (20 percent).[116] And according to a study by Bentley University, 84 percent of millennials said helping to make a positive difference in the world is more important than professional recognition. The Intelligence Group found similar results in its research. For instance, 64 percent of millennials said making the world a better place is a priority, and 88 percent said they want "work-life integration."

73%

Percentage of graduating students that said finding a job that allows them to do what they love was more important than finding a job that pays well

64%

Percentage of millennials that said making the world a better place is a priority

88%

Percentage of millennials that said they want "work-life integration"

84%

Percentage of millennials that said helping to make a positive difference in the world is more important than professional recognition

Rob Asghar, a *Forbes* contributor, summed it up this way: millennials are looking "strategically at opportunities to invest in a place where they can make a difference, preferably a place that itself makes a difference."[117]

This matters to leaders of all generations, because millennials are increasingly dominating the workforce. Consider that in 2015, millennials made up 33 percent of the US workforce [118] but by 2025, they are expected to make up more than 75 percent.[119] This generation includes more than 1.8 billion people worldwide, making it the largest generation alive.[120] Generation Z, meanwhile, already heavily influences consumer patterns and is making its way into the workforce.

These generation groups have never known a world without the internet or smartphones. Needless to say, they think and act differently than my generation. When I entered the workforce in the 1970s, I didn't ask why a company was in business or what purpose it served before taking a job. For that matter, it was hard to even learn much about a company other than what you read in published materials. Companies didn't have websites. There were no blogs about how an organization conducted business. There were no chat rooms that criticized management policy. I worked for whoever would hire me because I needed a job and because they paid me a regular check for doing what they wanted me to do. It was simple. It was transactional. I didn't ask many questions. I was loyal because they provided me work. That was what it took to satisfy me. And I expected nothing more.

Those days are gone. Companies don't just go out and hire people, especially talented people. They need to attract them. And as Meghan Biro, the CEO of TalentCulture, points out, they are attracted by purpose. Millennials, she wrote in a blog for the Huffington Post, expect transparency, value authenticity and access to power, and are quick to spot frauds.

"And most of all," she concluded, "millennials want employers to provide a sense of purpose.'"[121]

Gen Z, dubbed "true gen" by McKinsey & Company because the "search for truth" is at the root of its collective behaviors, differs from millennials in some ways, but also is highly motivated by causes they believe in.[122] They tend to be more pragmatic and realistic than millennials, according to McKinsey, but their behaviors are strongly tied to the purposes that attract them.

Michael Maccoby, a noted psychologist, leadership consultant, and author, says that purpose provides "a reason for asking others to follow or collaborate" and is an essential quality of a leader.[123] So, as a leader in modern climates, our role isn't just about making a profit and creating jobs; it's about making those jobs relevant...jobs that aren't just about financial reward, but that are about providing dignity, relevance, and purpose. And it can't be any purpose. It has to be a worthy, more noble purpose, one that grabs at the heart of people—a purpose that has a transformative influence on their lives, in their lives, and outside their lives.

THE SEARCH FOR PURPOSE

The responsibility for creating opportunities to serve and influence on a broader scale really began to hit home for me as we rebuilt Prologis during the financial crisis.

When I returned to Prologis, my thirty-minute commute to work each day became a time of great reflection on the "why?" questions pertaining to organizational purpose and work. There were days when I struggled with putting my finger on the real reason we needed to keep the company afloat. Why did we really need to turn the battleship in a different direction? Was it to save the jobs of the people who had labored there for years and years? Was it to perpetuate the brand? To save reputations? Or was it to avoid the embarrassment and hassle of sorting through bankruptcy?

The more I wrestled with such questions, the more I asked myself what we were in business to accomplish. Why did our people want to get up and go to work each day? Was it to make money and create financial prosperity? Was it to provide themselves with intellectual stimulation? Was it because they looked forward to social interactions they couldn't get at home?

Those are all valid reasons. But as I mentioned earlier, I believe people today crave something even more profound and powerful from their work. The climates we've discussed throughout this book are creating greater expectations as to what we all believe we and our companies should accomplish and why we should exist. As I considered my expectations for myself and for our organization, I realized I, too, wanted something more profound and powerful. In fact, I needed it.

Let me explain why.

Despite all the talk in recent years about "work-life balance," many of us spend more than half of our waking hours at work. Now, we may not be physically present at work for that long, but with smartphones, tablets, and all the other technology we have at our disposal thanks to the climate of accessibility, we have created an environment in which work is harder to avoid. More efficient? Yes. More demanding? No question about it! We are always connected. There is no excuse. On vacation, in the gym, on a golf course, in an airplane—we can always be found; we can always connect. Work dominates our time, whether we like it or not.

Emerging leaders can't afford to deny or avoid those realities as they shape their work environments and as they set examples for others to see. That's because those realities have helped reshape the definition of a "stakeholder" in the world's economy.

Like many leaders of my generation, I used to think the owner of a business was the most important stakeholder. The shareholder was at the top of the pyramid, and profits trumped all other motives. Milton Friedman, in his seminal 1962 book *Capitalism and Freedom*, said that in a free society, "there is one and only one social responsibility of business—to use its resources and engage in activities designed to increase its profits so long as it stays within the rules of the game, which is to say, engages in open and free competition without deception or fraud." He hammered that point home in a 1970 article for *The New York Times Magazine* aptly titled, "The Social Responsibility of Business is to Increase its Profits."

If you think that's old school in business thinking, consider the blunt approach of Turing Pharmaceuticals. I mentioned this company earlier, but its former CEO's approach to business is worth noting again here. When Turing acquired the drug Daraprim in August 2015 and promptly raised the price 5,000 percent, then-CEO Martin Shkreli took a great deal of heat from the public, the media, and Congress. But three months later he said his only regret was not raising the price more.

"I could have raised it higher and made more profits for our shareholders, which is my primary duty," Shkreli said during a *Forbes* Healthcare Summit. "No one wants to say it. No one's proud of it. But this is a capitalist society. Capitalist system. Capitalist rules. And my investors expect me to maximize profits. Not to minimize them or go half or go 70 percent. But to go to 100 percent of the profit curve."[124]

Within a few weeks of his appearance at the Healthcare Summit, Shkreli was arrested on charges of securities fraud and conspiracy in a case involving his previous job as a hedge fund manager. The charges had no direct connection to his work with Turing, but he stepped down as the company's CEO and eventually was convicted and sentenced to seven years in federal prison.

Shkreli's rise and fall paints a picture of capitalism at its worst—capitalism with no humility or heart.

Now, let's be clear: very few business leaders think or operate like Shkreli. But we're kidding ourselves if we think the desire to maximize profits doesn't drive many, if not most, business decisions around the world—and not just in capitalist countries. And while I never went anywhere near the extremes that Shkreli seems to favor, I did subscribe to Friedman's basic theory for the longest time and understood his logic. But more and more in today's climates, that way of thinking seems narrow and self-serving.

SHIFTING TO THE VALUE OF PURPOSE

So what approach is better?

I have heard leaders say that their sole purpose is to provide jobs for people so that those people can provide for their families and in turn create a better world. And I agree that this is a critically important purpose of any organization. But to me, that's like parents saying they can take care of all their child's needs by providing the shelter of a home. We all know that's simply not the case. It's a good start, but the responsibility doesn't end there. Yes, the owner or shareholder of a business is important. Yes, businesses exist to make money. Most businesses need to attract capital, and capital doesn't flow to folks that don't. And, yes, it's good that businesses provide jobs so people can make a living. But I think a better and broader objective of business is to create shareholder *value*.

Ahh.... Now, that's different. That objective requires more because it's not just about profits, it concerns the overall well-being of an organization. Any organization. A business, a nonprofit, a union, a government. They all represent congregations of people. And leaders will struggle to create value in today's climates without considering what their congregations desire. Why? Because their people are more integral to the success of the organization than ever. And the desires of their people are changing because of the ways they are shaped by the climates of access, diversity, and acceleration.

As leaders, however, we can't successfully drive shareholder value and organizational purpose if we haven't first found personal meaning in purpose that's outside of ourselves. Our purpose easily can center on ourselves—getting what we want, how we want it, and when we want it. A narcissist has purpose. But true meaning only comes from serving a purpose that's outwardly focused. A selfish personal purpose will never lead to a selfless organizational purpose.

Salesforce is a company that seems to understand the idea of creating shareholder value by connecting with a more noble purpose. CEO Marc

Benioff started the company in 1999 with a clear vision for creating a new business model based on technology but with a culture built on philanthropy. From the outset, he committed 1 percent of the company's equity, product, and time to a foundation. And new employees spend part of their first day on the job participating in a service project.

"I want a company where people are excited to come to work every day, where they feel good when they get here, where it doesn't take from them, but it's giving to them, it's giving to others," Benioff said in a 2018 interview with *The New York Times*. "Why do people want to be here? It's not that we have more amenities than everybody else. We have less. We don't have a cafeteria. But we have a stronger purpose and a stronger mission."[125]

Benioff dismisses the idea that companies can or should exist in some separated dominion from other parts of society.

"We need to have a more enlightened view about the role of companies," he said. "This company is not somehow separate from everything else. Are we not all connected? Are we not all one? Isn't that the point?"[126]

It's the outward focus, I believe, that's missing among many leaders in the world today, even many of those who beat their chest about changing the world. As the great Russian writer and philosopher Leo Tolstoy put it, "Everybody thinks of changing humanity, and nobody thinks of changing himself."[127] I believe leaders must take a look deep within themselves, connect to a noble purpose, and then discover how to pursue it in the context of their work and within the framework of their organizations.

Benioff started his company after a months-long sabbatical during which he met with spiritual gurus who helped him sort through his purpose in life. Many of my epiphanies came during the crucible of crisis, but it was a time steeped in reflection and prayer as I searched for answers. Some of those answers were found in two of the most influential books I've read in my life—*Halftime* by Bob Buford and *The Purpose Driven Life* by Rick Warren. Both took me out of the realm of myself and into the realm of others and how I could help them. In doing so, they helped me create more meaning in my life and helped me get out of my own way.

Warren points out that, "The only really happy people are those who have learned how to serve."[128] And, to be clear, he's talking about serving *others*.

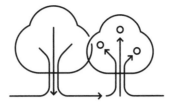

"MY FRUIT GROWS ON OTHER PEOPLE'S TREES."

BOB BUFORD

That, in fact, is how we discover our true purpose in life. "The search for the purpose of life has puzzled people for thousands of years," Warren writes. "That's because we typically begin at the wrong starting point—ourselves. We ask self-centered questions like 'What do I want to be? What do I want to do with my life? What are *my* goals, *my* ambitions, *my* dreams for *my* future?' But focusing on ourselves will never reveal our life's purpose."[129]

When our purpose includes serving others, we find meaning in their accomplishments. As Buford put it, "My fruit grows on other people's trees." That's the fruit of significance, which is far more valuable than success. "Success means using your knowledge and experience to satisfy yourself," Buford said. "Significance means using your knowledge and experience to change the lives of others."

That's the type of transfluent purpose I seek for my life.

RAISING EXPECTATIONS

Not only do employees expect more from their employers, but so does everyone who is connected to the organization. You see, our world of glass houses has raised the bar: the more people understand about an organization, the more they expect.

The best way I know how to explain this is by relating it to the courtship of my wife. The first time we met, Sue had no expectations of me or our relationship. And, in fact, her initial impressions of me probably weren't that good. We were on a chartered flight with a number of business associates, and Sue had come along as a guest of one of my customers. During the flight, a friend and I were clowning around a bit. Long story and I'll spare you the details, but it involved pillowcases and sunglasses. And a few too many drinks.

Somehow, I overcame that first impression, and Sue eventually agreed to go out with me.

Our expectations of each other and of the relationship on those first few dates remained simple. She expected me to treat her with respect and to do things like open the car door for her. Meanwhile, I wondered if she was a Steelers fan. After about five dates, however, our conversations had grown deeper, more transparent. She knew there was more to me than that guy she first saw dancing in the aisles of an airplane with a pillowcase pulled over his head. I knew there was more to her than an attractive and successful businesswoman. By this point, we had shared our values, our hopes, and our dreams. And we had seen how those things impacted our decisions and behaviors. The more transparent we were with each other, the more we strengthened our trust in each other. Our feelings ran deeper, and our expectations of each other and for the relationship began to grow.

I think the same is true for organizations in today's climates. Our personal and organizational values, strategies, and expectations are open to anyone and everyone who has an interest—so are our decisions and behaviors. The more people know about us and like what they see, the more they feel a connection to who we are and what we're doing. And the greater the connection, the greater their expectations of who we should be and how we should behave. Think about companies that are well known for opening themselves up to the world around them—companies like Starbucks, TOMS, or the Container Store. Even if you don't agree with all of their policies and practices, you have certain expectations of them—higher expectations, most likely—because you know what they say they believe, you've seen how they live their stated values, and you've seen the value they provide to others.

Transfluence provides a framework and mindset for creating and then living up to these increased expectations, but it also creates a rising tide for even more. The more your leadership exemplifies transfluence, the more you achieve the broader business objective of creating shareholder value. With that comes even greater expectations—first for you as a leader and then for your entire organization. As the wave of trust builds, the entire organization has opportunities to accomplish transfluence—to see its transformative influence flow outward and create greater and more lasting value.

This is how a more noble purpose continually grows bigger and broader.

Again, I would argue adding real value to society isn't just an opportunity, it's an obligation.

This was the conclusion I eventually came to during all those morning commutes: that organizations should exist for something bigger, broader, and more powerful than providing products and services, providing workers with a paycheck, or making a profit. They should exist to create value through transfluence. That value comes from knowing and pursuing meaning through purpose—the things that matter to your employees, to your community, and to the homeless second-grader with big, brown eyes.

CHAPTER RECAP

Transformative influence is at its highest level when leaders impact the lives of those they lead and that influence multiplies to benefit others. As human beings, we crave purpose and meaning in our lives. A core responsibility of a transfluent leader is not only to provide opportunities for others to excel in their work but also to provide meaning in what they do.

TRANSFLUENCE IN ACTION

+ Take a look at your work environment. Do people see meaning and purpose in what they do? There are multiple opportunities around you to create and enhance meaning and purpose. Look for them and act on them.

GUIDEPOST NO. 10

MAINTAINING PASSION
IS HARD WORK.

RE-IGNITE IT DAILY.

14.

➡ PASSION: EARTH, WIND, AND FIRE

I WANTED TO DO SOMETHING THAT HADN'T BEEN DONE BEFORE.
– MAURICE WHITE[130]

More than forty inches of rain fell across parts of southern Texas during a four-day span in late August 2017. Wind gusts topped out at more than 130 miles per hour in the gulf coast town of Port Aransas. Streets in many cities, including Houston, looked like canals, as an estimated thirty thousand people left their homes for higher and safer ground.

By the time the wind and rain had done their damage, eighty-nine people had died, most from drownings, and the storm had inflicted an estimated $125 billion in damages. The most enduring legacy of Hurricane Harvey, however, isn't in how much it destroyed, but in what it revealed—example after example of transfluent leaders. In the midst of the costliest hurricane on record—and is so often the case when tragedy strikes—men and women worked courageously to have a transformative influence on the battered world around them. First responders rescued nearly twenty thousand people during the storm. Ordinary citizens sacrificed their time, possessions, and energy to help total strangers who were in need. And some of the area's best-known residents stepped forward, leading the effort to raise money to rebuild homes, businesses, and lives and to replace despair with hope for the future.

When the flooding began, for instance, Jim "Mattress Mack" McIngvale posted a video online inviting shelter-seekers to come to one of his two showrooms. His inventory of brand-new recliners, sofas, and love seats quickly became resting spots for the displaced. He even used his delivery trucks and their drivers to shuttle in people who were stranded in their homes.[131]

When four employees of El Bolillo Bakery found themselves marooned at work, they decided to make the most of it. They still had electricity and all the ingredients they needed for *pan dulce* (a Mexican sweet bread), so they went to work turning 4,400 pounds of flour into hundreds of loaves of bread to feed the hungry in their community.[132]

When professional golfer Stacy Lewis first saw televised news reports about the storm, she was preparing to leave Ottawa, Canada, for the Cambia Portland Classic in Oregon, her next stop on the LPGA Tour. By the time she reached Oregon, her hometown of Houston resembled a swamp. She said she felt "helpless in Portland" and "needed to give myself a purpose for being there."[133] So, in a quick decision after talking to her husband, she committed to donate whatever she won that weekend to help victims of the hurricane.

Lewis said she felt more nervous about the idea of playing poorly than about what that commitment might cost her financially. As it happened, she played some of her best golf in years. That's saying a lot for someone who had won, to that point, more than $12 million in her career. When the story leaked out, it caught the attention of the golf world, especially as Lewis fought her way to victory—the twelfth title of her LPGA career but the first in a little more than three years. As promised, she donated the $195,000 prize. One of her sponsors, KPMG, matched that donation, and some of her friends anonymously chipped in another $60,000.

The most famous fund-raiser, of course, was J.J. Watt. The all-pro defensive lineman for the Houston Texans went to social media with a goal of raising $200,000 for the relief effort and wound up pulling in $37 million from more than two hundred thousand donors. Peter King, the long-time NFL writer for *Sports Illustrated*, pointed out that, "Nothing J.J. Watt has achieved in his career, or might still achieve, will measure up to what he did for Houston."[134]

Another famous athlete, Jose Altuve of the Houston Astros, made a different type of contribution. Yes, he pledged more than $30,000 to the recovery and arranged for one of his sponsors to provide $25,000 worth of shoes, but there was much more to his story. When the Astros returned home for the first time after the storms, Altuve and several teammates went to some of the shelters and visited with people who had lost everything they owned.

"I felt bad," he told Sports Illustrated. "But in the middle of all that disaster we were able to still see smiles on their faces. I said to myself, 'These people are going through a really tough time, and they're still able to smile. And you're able to give them hope.' That's what it's all about: helping each other. The city of Houston has treated me really good since I got to the big leagues. And I felt that I owed them something. They made me the player I am by supporting me every day. So, when they were having a hard time, I wanted to give something back to them."[135]

At five-foot-six, Altuve had been considered too small for professional baseball, but he had worked his way into an MVP and was just the type of inspirational model of perseverance Houston needed as he helped the Astros to their first World Series title in franchise history. Throughout the playoffs, he provided constant reminders that he and his teammates were playing for more than a ring, for more than the glory, for more than a place in history—they were playing for Houston.

Watt and Altuve shared Sports Illustrated's "Sportsperson of the Year" award for 2017, largely because they led by speaking "loudest in their actions and words off the field."[136]

Physicists typically put forces of nature into four categories—gravity, electromagnetism, the strong nuclear force, and the weak nuclear force. The rest of us tend to think of things related to earth, wind, fire, and water— things like hurricanes, earthquakes, floods, and wildfires. I think of a force of nature, however, as someone whose passion for creating a transformative influence won't be slowed by the elements around them. That's what I saw in the aftermath of Hurricane Harvey—in Watt, Altuve, Lewis, the employees of El Bolillo Bakery, Jim "Mattress Mack" McIngvale, and countless others. They not only were driven by a purpose, but they had a passion that was overwhelming. And that's what I see in many emerging leaders around the world—they want to have a transformative influence with their leadership, and nothing will stand in their way.

Transfluent leaders, however, are a force of nature in everyday life, not just during high-profile events. There is a consistency that others should see in their thoughts, words, and actions. When tragedies or tough times strike, that consistency provides the foundation for a courageous, effective response—as was the case in the heroes who emerged from Hurricane Harvey. So, as we move toward the close of our discussion about transfluence, we will look at the profound power of a passion that creates a consistent daily influence and makes us a force of nature as leaders, regardless of whether times are great or if disasters are darkening our doorways.

SUFFERING FOR PURPOSE

The word passion elicits an emotional response for most of us. We connect it very quickly to something, and that something is often personal—something we've read, something we've seen, something we've experienced, something we hope to experience.

We might immediately put it in a romantic context and think of a white-hot encounter between lovers in a movie. Or we might connect it to something we love—a hobby, our work, a prized possession, an important cause, our spouse. We can have passion in a relationship, but we also can have a passion for driving fast cars, for listening to opera, for collecting fine wine, for playing golf (guilty), or for traveling the world (double guilty). And we can have a passion for things like helping people in need or for building an amazing culture in our companies.

If all of that makes passion sound like nothing but fun and games, keep in mind that the original definition of passion involves suffering. It comes from the Latin words *pati* (to suffer) and *passio* (suffering, being acted upon). This is why the "Passion of the Christ" refers to the suffering Jesus experienced between the Last Supper and His crucifixion. Passion, in other words, involves a *willingness* to suffer in pursuit of something that's important and valuable. It doesn't mean that suffering is inevitable, but it means that the commitment to sacrifice of ourselves is there and clearly evident in our actions.

I'm not talking about the passion of a fan who sits on the couch or in the stands, buys merchandise with the team logo, cheers enthusiastically when things go well, and complains loudly when thing go poorly. I'm talking about the men and women who step onto the field of play and truly risk something. Who willingly sacrifice time, money, energy, and ego. Who put themselves out there for the sake of others. And if it doesn't work out—and sometimes even when it does—they lose something that mattered to them.

It's that type of commitment—that all-in willingness to sacrifice for the object of our passion—that creates the intense fire and overwhelming resolve we need to fuel our purpose and to energize people around us. Without real passion, our purpose inevitably is weakened. We won't rise to meet the opportunities that come with our purpose, and we won't persevere against the storms that threaten it. But when we have genuine, intense passion, our purpose comes alive, and it transforms us and everyone around us.

The passion of a transfluent leader can take many forms, but it's always tied to a higher and noble purpose. It always connects to serving others. It might emerge during a fiery speech to rally the troops, it might show up in the steely resolve during a tough negotiation, or it might speak softly in the simple but powerful examples of quietly going above and beyond to help someone in need. It burns regardless of whether it has an audience. Its oxygen isn't applause, it's action.

WAKE UP, KID

John O'Leary experienced the benefits of an activated passion when one of his childhood heroes was inspired to make a transformative influence on his life.

O'Leary literally was playing with fire one day in the garage of his family's St. Louis home. It was 1987, and he was just nine years old when he lit a piece of cardboard and accidentally caused a gas can to explode. He was rushed to the hospital with third-degree burns over his entire body and less than a 1 percent chance of surviving through the night. Two days later, as he lay strapped to a bed and unable to speak or see, O'Leary heard a familiar voice at his bedside.

"Kid, wake up," the voice said. "You're going to live. You are going to survive. Keep fighting."

It was the late, great Hall of Fame broadcaster Jack Buck, the voice of O'Leary's beloved St. Louis Cardinals baseball team.

Buck and O'Leary had no previous connection. But Red Schoendienst, a veteran coach with the Cardinals, had heard about O'Leary's story from his daughter, and he mentioned it to Buck during a charity event. He told Buck he was headed out of town the next morning, but he planned to visit O'Leary when he returned because he knew O'Leary was a huge Cardinals fan. Moved by the story, Buck decided to make a visit of his own the next day.

As he was leaving O'Leary's bedside, Buck broke down in tears, and that was before he was told there was little chance O'Leary would survive. Buck didn't give up, however, and he wouldn't let O'Leary give up, either. He replaced fear with certainty. Then he backed his faith with actions. He went home and asked himself a profound question: *what more can I do?* And for the next five months, Buck returned almost daily to O'Leary's bedside with the same message.

"Wake up, kid. You are going to live. Keep fighting."

Buck even told O'Leary that the Cardinals were going to hold "John O'Leary Day" after the boy recovered. And in July 1987, O'Leary was rolled into the old Busch Memorial Stadium, strapped into a wheelchair, his fingers gone from amputation, for "John O'Leary Day."

Two days later, he received a package in the mail. It was a baseball signed by another future Hall of Famer, shortstop Ozzie Smith. It came with a note from Buck.

"Kid, if you want a second baseball," the note said, "all you have to do is write a thank-you note to the guy who sent the first."

Buck knew O'Leary had no fingers and couldn't write. But, O'Leary said, "I think he also knew the power of inspiration and the power of connectivity." [137]

The note indeed inspired O'Leary. With some help from his parents, he scribbled out a barely legible thank-you note and mailed it to Ozzie Smith. Soon thereafter, as promised, he got another signed ball—and another note from Buck with the same challenge and the same promise. He wrote another thank-you note, and he got another ball. Then another. And another. By the end of that summer, O'Leary had collected sixty signed baseballs. And even though he had no fingers, he had learned to write again.

Buck and O'Leary stayed in touch over the years. And on the night O'Leary graduated from Saint Louis University, Buck sent him a graduation present—the crystal baseball Buck had received when he was inducted into the Hall of Fame. It was the ultimate symbol of Buck's professional accomplishments in life, and yet he gave it away.

O'Leary went on to get married, have four kids, become a successful businessman, and establish himself as a sought-after motivational speaker.

His oldest son's name? Jack. His book, *On Fire*, tells the full story about Buck and many others who helped him overcome the obstacles he faced in the days, months, and years following the accident—the people who looked outside their storms, who lived with purpose, and who had the passion to sacrifice for the good of others.

"Do we understand the importance of our mentorship, of our leadership, of our love into the lives of others?" O'Leary asks in a video on his website. "I wonder sometimes. Because this man's life changed mine. He gave me something to believe in during a very, very difficult time."[138] [139]

Buck's passion for helping O'Leary led him to action. Action with meaning in purpose. Action that was selfless and sacrificial. Action that wasn't focused on himself or his own storms. Actions that had a transformative influence on the life of someone he previously didn't even know.

WILDFIRES

So what happens when transfluent leaders consistently display genuine passion for a meaningful purpose? I believe at least three things result. One, their purpose spreads. Two, their passion expands. And, three, the purpose and passion of everyone around them expands. They create uncontainable wildfires of purpose and passion that become a force of nature.

When transfluent leaders are driven by their personal passions, they tap into and galvanize the organizational passions of their people. They connect their passion to their work and the passions of their employees to the company's purpose, and then they make sure it's evident in every aspect of how they do business. Buck's passion for helping O'Leary, for instance, not only helped in O'Leary's recovery, but it inspired countless people within the Cardinals' organization and throughout the St. Louis community. And O'Leary continues to spread that passion for helping others through his book and his speaking career.

But passion isn't just about inspiration that leads to on-the-spot actions. It also takes root to create sustained actions—policies, programs, and events that feed on passion but that also feed the passion.

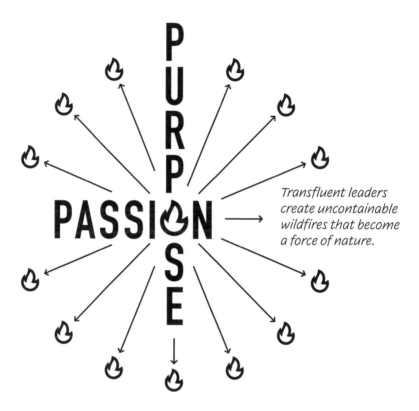

Transfluent leaders create uncontainable wildfires that become a force of nature.

At Prologis, we had a global workforce—people who lived and worked all over the planet and who had different cultural norms and varying interests. In thinking about our common areas of passion, one of the things that struck us early on was the excitement that our younger employees and their international colleagues had for the environment. In fact, it was the most important thing to many in our European workforce.

Now, I'm not an environmentalist, nor do I profess to be an expert on global warming or climate change. But we tried to look at it logically, which is all executives can do. And we concluded that if we could do our part in contributing to the environment in a positive way, we should. Why? Because no matter what we individually believed about global warming, we knew protecting the environment was a good thing to do, and it was important to our employees, to the communities we operated in, and, as we were to later find out, to our customers. So, it had to become an integral part of our strategic plan.

That's what led us to create solar energy from the rooftops of our buildings. At the time, we owned more than five hundred million square feet of rooftop space, which I'm pretty sure was more than anyone other than the governments of Russia and China. Those rooftops were a non-income producing asset. They couldn't be rented, and they cost us money to periodically repair. But there was a hidden potential in these assets; the same sun that causes damage just happens to be a giant ball of energy constantly shining on the roofs of our facilities. So, in 2005 we created a program to begin covering some of our rooftops with solar panels and selling the electricity into the power grid. It wasn't easy at first because the cost of providing solar at that time was expensive. But our efforts prevailed and today, as the price of solar continues to fall, the company has developed more than 186 megawatts of generating capacity in nine countries. That's enough to power nearly thirty thousand homes each year.

We also were one of the largest, if not the largest, property developers in the world. In any one year, it would not be uncommon for us to build two hundred new buildings, each one averaging three US football fields long by one football field wide. That's more than fifty million square feet of new space globally at a cost of more than $3 billion annually. We were the poster child for facilitating globalization. Given the size of our operation, we knew we had a responsibility to do it right, not because it was required but because we had a conscience.

We started by measuring the environmental output of our development process, and that led to changes in the way we operated. We set goals and objectives. We started constructing buildings by sourcing local and regional construction materials. We began recycling all of our waste, installing energy efficient lighting, using high-performance glass, and providing water-efficient landscaping. We spent extra money to educate and certify our workforce. We partnered with our suppliers to educate them. And we made sure we surpassed the highest environmental ratings achievable in every part of the world that we operated in. We also appointed champions in each city to study best practices to ensure our operations were as efficient as possible.

In short, we not only had a transformative influence on our communities, we transformed the hearts and minds of our people by tapping into their passions. In doing so, we created a tremendous amount of pride and goodwill throughout our workforce.

Amazingly, what set out to be a desire for greater organizational purpose became a growing pulse in our company. Our executives were speaking all over the world about our efforts. Much of what we talked about was picked up on social media. Awareness grew, and people were writing about our environmentally conscious company. Equity indexes that invested in socially responsible companies began including us, which positively impacted the liquidity of our stock. And, most importantly, we became the preferred provider to many of our customers who believed in the importance of corporate responsibility.

While at first glance a topic like purpose may not connect with the bottom line, research by Rodgers Palmer and Bill Schaninger of McKinsey & Company proves exactly that point. They have studied thirty-seven workplace practices based on more than five million survey responses representing employees at 1,700 organizations. The result: nine outcomes for a metric measuring organizational health. And here's their key conclusion: organizational health, supported by a sense of meaning and well-being, correlates with financial performance.

"Whether the relationship between individual and organizational health is causal or merely correlated, we don't yet know," they wrote in an article for *McKinsey Quarterly*. "Nor do we particularly care. The facts before us suggest that meaning, health, and performance go hand in hand—and that should be enough for leaders seeking to leave a legacy by improving their companies and the lives of their employees."[140]

We certainly found this to be the case at Prologis. Despite the tough financial environment, our development business was growing by hundreds of millions of dollars each year due in large part to what we stood for and what we could uniquely deliver to our customers. Our customers wanted environmentally efficient buildings, and they knew we were the experts in providing them. Not only did our efforts fuel pride in our organization, but they were paying dividends in our profitability.

We were excited that our employees were excited about what we were doing as a company, but we also wanted to give them opportunities to express their individual passions in very tangible, personal ways. Passion isn't just something you watch and applaud; it has to be active in your life, or it slowly fades. So, we also looked for ways to engage our workforce in regular activities that allowed them to express their passions in influential ways.

Again, given the diverse points of view from throughout the world, creating a common theme wasn't easy. When I interviewed employees in the US and UK, they generally understood the direction we wanted to move, and they immediately gravitated toward areas where we could serve the less fortunate. But in France, our people thought I was nuts. At first, they couldn't understand why this was our responsibility. In their eyes, the government was responsible. That's why they paid taxes! When we introduced the notion that perhaps they could hold bike races to raise awareness for certain causes, however, they got more excited. The French are passionate about road biking! And in Japan, we were challenged by the fact that it wasn't traditional to give to others who are weaker. In fact, it would be odd for someone to even accept help. But as soon as they knew they could hold clean up days in each city we operated in, they got more excited. The Japanese respect cleanliness!

In every office throughout the world, we encouraged and empowered people to think creatively and do whatever they thought would have the biggest impact in their backyard. We promised to support them financially, but only if they contributed their time to the cause. We didn't write checks without the sweat of our employees working together toward a common goal. This was not a campaign to raise money for the United Way; this was an effort to change the hearts of our people and add value to their lives and their communities. And everyone in every city in the world needed to have a cause. Something they could be passionate about. Something that was outward focused. Something that was authentic. Something that showed their honesty. Something that introduced humility. And something that showed they were human and had a heart for others.

Our people were unleashed like they had never been before. We did everything from building schools in China to working on houses for Habitat for Humanity. We established a global "Space for Good" program where we donated empty warehouse space for disaster relief efforts and other community causes. We contributed time to local hospitals in Warsaw and inner-city youth organizations in Denver. We organized and participated in awareness races in the UK and spent time in elderly care facilities in Germany. We stored toys for children for the holidays in our warehouses throughout the US. We built football fields and playgrounds for kids in Bucharest. We even built a memorial for a World War II pilot who heroically redirected his damaged aircraft and saved innocent lives in doing so.

Not only did we empower our associates to do these things, but we also recognized them for their efforts. We spent a significant part of every town hall meeting showcasing teams of people from throughout the world, many times in bandanas and jeans doing something impactful. Sometimes we all just cheered, and sometimes it got emotional. Many times, I couldn't hold back tears in front of employees. You could literally feel the passion during these presentations.

We also wanted our people to know we cared about them as much as we cared about impacting others. We gave them paid time off, not only to work on their office cause, but also to work on their own charitable passion. We created a matching gift program to provide funds that would help them support their favorite organizations financially. We created a dollars-for-doers program to compensate those organizations even more depending on the time our employees worked there. And we provided a foundational grant program that offered additional financial support for those organizations focused in certain targeted areas.

We wanted our people to know that it was important to us that they provided leadership in their spheres of influence. We understood that it was through selflessness that our people would achieve their greatest accomplishments and that selflessness would have a dramatic effect on their lives and the lives of those they touched every day.

We placed so much importance on these efforts that we set up a separate committee of our board of directors to help hold us accountable and monitor our progress. You can't force passion, but I believe strongly in measurement and accountability. Nothing gets sustained attention in organizations unless it gets reported on and people are held accountable for it. Our board was sympathetic to what we needed to do to run a 21st century company with a workforce that wanted meaning in purpose and a management team that wanted to be responsive to it. In addition to setting up the board committee, we also became the first in our industry to publish annual results on our social and environmental activities. These things made serving others a part of our DNA at every level of the organization.

I'm obviously proud of what our employees accomplished at Prologis, but I'm especially proud that we had a management team and board that was passionate about making such a profound difference in the lives of their employees and the communities we served. When leaders are passionate about having a transformative influence on the lives of people, it creates a fire that burns throughout their organizations. It's a force of nature that can't be controlled.

Your organization doesn't look like Prologis, so it will face the climates of our culture with its own unique strengths and weaknesses. But the principles of transfluence are universal. They're built on timeless values that any leader of any organization of any size and in any place can implement consistently over time and reasonably expect similar results—a transformative influence for the higher purpose of modern business.

Personally, I can't wait to see what you do next.

CHAPTER RECAP

Passion provides the fuel for purpose and meaning. It requires an all-in willingness to sacrifice for the commitment. And it always connects to serving others. You become a force of nature when your passion for creating a transformative influence won't be slowed by the elements around you. When you are passionate about having a transformative influence on the lives of people, it creates a fire that burns throughout your organization. It's a force of nature that can't be controlled.

TRANSFLUENCE IN ACTION

+ Be a transformative influence to those around you and make sure you do it by providing meaning and purpose with a massive amount of passion in all you do. Good luck!

EPILOGUE

The story of Prologis and the story of my leadership philosophy intertwined for nearly two decades, climaxing during those final years when the future of the company was on the line. Both were refined by the fires of adversity and emerged better and stronger than ever.

This book, of course, focused on the leadership part of the story and, more specifically, on the principles I believe will serve next-generation leaders in our complex and ever-changing climates. And while I leaned heavily on my Prologis experiences, you might be wondering what happened to the company.

When I returned to Prologis as CEO, we knew we had to pay off at least $2 billion in debt to buy credibility in the market. We also knew we had to create enough income to buy time on our debt covenants. And we knew we had to do these things quickly. So, after hours and hours of hand-wringing and stone-turning, our people came up with what proved to be a brilliant solution—selling our entire business in China and some of our business in Japan for approximately $1.5 billion. It seemed like a drastic decision, and the market certainly thought it was. But we knew a buyer who wanted it, we desperately needed the cash, and we knew we would book a fairly significant gain on the sale that would help buy us the necessary time with our creditors. We also felt confident we could rebuild whatever we lost in a better way in the future. So, we did it and never looked back.

Then, from 2009 through the end of 2010, we reorganized the company, generated additional cash by selling more than $7 billion in assets (that's more than one thousand buildings), bought back more than a billion dollars of our bonds at massive discounts, raised $3 billion of new equity, restructured our covenants, and paid off more than $10 billion of debt.

We did a plethora of other things, as well. We cut our dividends to save cash, and we took steps to significantly reduce the operating risk in the company. We leased more than 90 percent of our speculative developments, which substantially increased our cash flow, but we also closed some fringe operations in India and Brazil. We had to cut overhead, which meant we had to lay off a third of our workforce, re-organize our senior management team, and let go of four of the top ten people in the company. We tried to save jobs, but we realized the only way we could save the company was by shedding payroll expenses. That was hard.

In short, we applied sound business practices and, in concert with the cultural changes, we put the company on a different trajectory.

Once we got through the initial storms and felt confident Prologis again was strong and healthy, I set my sights on two main objectives—positioning the company for sustained success in its long-term future and positioning myself for retirement as CEO.

The truth is, I never held ambitions for running the company. I took the job, as I said from the beginning, because I loved the people, believed in the positive influence Prologis could have, and wanted to do all I could to help it emerge from the devastating effects of the recession. I was still young—in my mid-fifties—but the crisis leadership phase of life had taken a toll on me and my family. I was ready for something new, and Prologis deserved a leader with a long-term time horizon.

So, in 2011, we completed the largest merger in the history of the real estate industry when we joined forces with AMB Property Corporation, who at the time was our biggest competitor. Hamid Moghadam, the CEO of AMB and one of its co-founders, joined me as co-CEO of the company for a transitional year, and then, as prearranged, I stepped aside. Hamid remains chairman and CEO of Prologis, which still has a presence in Denver but now has its headquarters in San Francisco.

Prologis once again is among the strongest companies on the planet. In fact, it is the largest industrial real estate company in the world.[141] Just as importantly, it continues to strengthen its commitment to its people and the communities where it operates—and not just for its 1,600 employees, but for the more than seven hundred thousand people around the world who work inside facilities owned by Prologis.

In recent years, for instance, the company has taken its philanthropy to a higher level by launching a Community Workforce Initiative. They partner with international and local NGOs to invest in workforce education and training for the underserved populations in the cities where they operate.

This initiative is creating a broader, more diverse, and high-skilled talent pool for their customers and providing new opportunities for groups who are historically marginalized. The program already is in major markets in the US, UK, and Mexico, with plans to scale it globally and a goal of helping train twenty-five thousand individuals by 2025. That's powerful influence at work!

The transformation of Prologis from its near-death experience to the picture of corporate fitness certainly qualifies as a success story worthy of telling. What I learned through that process, however, is where I see even greater value, especially for leaders in the modern economy. Pushing the right buttons and pulling the right levers were essential to our survival, but it wasn't enough for sustained success. It also required a commitment to each other and to the company that was found from the lowest-paid employee to the top of the organizational chart. And while we didn't label it this way at the time, that commitment exemplified transfluence—an organization filled with leaders who were using adversity in our lives to make a positive difference in the lives of others.

Adversity is really strange. No one wants to go through it, and yet it is such a powerful change agent when channeled the right way. Adversity caused our leadership team to think creatively, act boldly, and develop the traits that are essential to transfluence. The English essayist William Hazlitt once wrote that, "Prosperity is a great teacher; adversity is a greater [teacher]."[142] No kidding! I often told our employees that adversity causes us to persevere and that perseverance builds character. And I can tell you that I learned more in 2008 through 2010 than I have in any other three-year period. It was the toughest time of my life, but it strengthened my character and shaped the way I thought about leading.

A few years after I stepped away from Prologis, a friend sent me a note after listening to Dave Butts speak at a business leaders' luncheon. Butts has a remarkable story about surviving stage 4 cancer, and he was talking about how leaders faced with adversity need an inner peace that's bigger than the chaos of the world around them. That inner peace, he said, is what attracts people to follow a leader.

"We don't get to choose the circumstances around us," he said, "but we do have a choice about what's going on inside of us."[143]

When we make the choice to deal with our demons, act in alignment with our core values, and lead from an "it's not about me" perspective, it positions us for something greater. Something sustainable. Something that lives on even when we're gone. That's when we can ignite others to do great things and truly have a transformational influence in the lives of those we touch.

ACKNOWLEDGMENTS

This book is about creating transformative influence in the lives of those we lead. And, as you might expect, a great number of people have had a transformative influence on my life throughout the years. Unfortunately, the list is too long to even begin to name everyone whose influence has in some way shaped the content of this book—my close friends, business associates, fellow board members, men's fellowship groups, family members, and many others. I owe you all a great deal of gratitude.

Among the people involved most directly with the book, let me start by thanking Anthony Ziccardi and Maddie Sturgeon at Post Hill Press, Ken Gillett and his team at Target Marketing, and Mark Fortier and his team at Fortier Public Relations. Your professionalism and hard work in publishing and marketing this book was invaluable to me as a first-time author.

And then there is my team. When I retired from Prologis, I set out to build a team that could help me to accomplish what I couldn't accomplish on my own. I needed people who could help me think through concepts and ideas, write those thoughts in a way that others could understand, and make sure it was done in a format that others could relate to. I needed research, literary, and media capabilities. I needed people to bounce ideas off of and delegate responsibilities to. I needed people who could help me create and maintain a website and make sure we were writing about relevant topics in blogs and other materials leading up to the book release.

Thank God, I found that team! I could not be more delighted to have Antonella Iannarino, Stephen Caldwell, Denise McMahan, Michael Palgon, and Tony Steck as partners. Thank you for all of your contributions. You have gelled into a great unit, and your work and influence on me and this process has been nothing short of stellar! I also want to thank Suzanne Dawson, Rick Keating, and Bill Fallon for their work early on in helping me sculpt what the book should look like. This book would not be what it is without each of you.

And then, of course, there are people who affirmed, sometimes challenged, and certainly influenced the things I had to say. Special thanks go to John Mack, Frank Blake, David Alexander, and Debbie Cafaro, CEOs who led corporate turn-arounds of great companies; to Joe Sanders, who leads one of the best run inner-city youth organizations in America; to Tom Melton, a consultant and former pastor who especially helped me think through fear and pride; and to Tommy Spaulding, who has written two New York Times bestsellers on relationships and heart-led leadership. All of you have been blessed with profound experiences and wisdom that shaped my thinking and influenced me greatly. Thank you again for your friendship and the time you spent with me.

I also cannot forget my associates at Prologis. During my twenty years there, I had the unique opportunity to meet some of the greatest people I will ever know in more than a hundred cities around the world—places like Denver, Chicago, Columbus, San Francisco, El Paso, Tokyo, Shanghai, Mexico City, São Paulo, Birmingham, Paris, Amsterdam, Dusseldorf, Luxembourg, Milan, and Prague. I cannot possibly thank all of you by name, those who are still with the company and those, like me, who have moved on. But your support and dedication to the organization and to me has meant a lot over the years. Because of you, I am proud to say that I was a part of one of the greatest organizations that has existed on the planet—and you continue to make it even better.

A special thanks goes to Bill Sullivan, Ted Antenucci, Ed Nekritz, and Gary Anderson, my senior management team at Prologis. You kept me focused during 2008 and 2009 when we were on the ropes. Looking back, I could not have picked four better people to be in the trenches with as we worked through the challenges that we faced. You were nothing short of amazing, and we all have some battle scars to show for it!

I also want to say a special thanks to my mother, Josephine, my father, Walter, and my sisters, Julianne Rakowich-Rose and Mary Jane McCall. Mom and Dad are no longer with us, but I was fortunate to have parents who lived transfluent lives. I never met a person who didn't love my parents. They were hardworking, unassuming children of first-generation immigrants who loved others and were net-givers to society. They were as selfless and honest as the day is long. And my sisters and I went to school on them every day. Today, my sisters and I love and respect each other. We help each other. We care about each other. We saw what transformative influence was all about just by the way Mom and Dad lived their lives. Thank you, Mom and Dad, for who you were. Julie, Mary, and I try to be like you every day. You were the best role models kids could ever ask for, and this book is as much your legacy as mine.

Finally, I want to thank the three people closest to me: my wife and children. My daughter Nicole and son Matthew are my pride and joy. Words cannot express the influence you have had on my life. Nicole, you are a model of transparency, and Matt, your fearlessness is contagious! My sense is that you have more to teach me now than I have to teach you. So bring it on! And, of course, where would I be without Sue, my wife of thirty-one years? Sue, you have brought me incredible joy and happiness, and you have been there for me through ups and downs and sometimes sideways, too. I could not have written this book without the incredible love and support you have always provided me. You are, hands down, the best wife a guy could have! And I love you dearly.

Oh, and one last thank-you to make. That is to my God. During the times I struggled the most, You were there. And the cool thing about You is that You make sure I learn the most in the toughest times in my life. You are my rock— always have been and always will be. You give my life meaning and purpose. You are the epitome of transformative influence. Thank you for providing me with wisdom during this journey. It is much appreciated!

APPENDIX

10 FUNDAMENTAL GUIDEPOSTS FOR TRANSFLUENCE

1. Harsh climates bring tough challenges. Embrace every one of them.

2. Storms rage from deep within us and confronting them is painful.
   Endure the pain.

3. Fear and pride can drive the decisions of leaders. Don't give them control.

4. Selfishness is our default response as humans. Be selfless and different.

5. Transparency is scary and uncomfortable. Be bold and let people in.

6. Humility puts our pride at risk. Risk it anyway.

7. Honesty often leads to conflict. Never waiver from the battle.

8. Leading with heart requires trust. Give trust a chance.

9. Purpose and meaning are fleeting. Never give up on them.

10. Maintaining passion is hard work. Re-ignite it daily.

ENDNOTES

1   Henry Melvill, "Partaking in Other Men's Sins," (address, St. Margaret's Church, Lothbury, England, June 12, 1855); also printed in *Golden Lectures*, 1855

2   "Einstein Is Terse in Rule for Success," *The New York Times*, June 20, 1932, https://www.nytimes.com/1932/06/20/archives/einstein-is-terse-in-rule-for-success-only-life-lived-for-others-is.html

3   Kent M. Keith, "The Origin of The Paradoxical Commandments," www.paradoxicalcommandments.com/origin/ (Accessed May 10, 2018)

4   Twitter, June 2, 2012, https://twitter.com/paulocoelho/status/209008454948495360

5   Marcus Aurelius, Meditations, Book VII, 167 A.C.E., http://classics.mit.edu/Antoninus/meditations.7.seven.html

6   George Rawlinson, *The History of Herodotus: A New English Version, Volume II* (D. Appleton and Company, 1889)

7   Jon Gordon, "The Law of the Skyscraper," *Jon Gordon's Weekly Newsletter*, January 12, 2014

8   Joseph Demakis, *The Ultimate Book of Quotations* (CreateSpace, November 19, 2012)

9   This quote is often attributed to Mark Twain, but like so many of his quotes, there's not much proof he actually said it.

10   Andrew Perrin and Madhu Kumar, "About three-in-ten U.S. adults say they are 'almost constantly' online," Pew Research, July 25, 2019, http://www.pewresearch.org/fact-tank/2019/07/25/americans-going-online-almost-constantly/ (Accessed November 12, 2019)

11   Steve Morgan, "Humans On The Internet Will Triple From 2015 To 2022 And Hit 6 Billion," *Cybercrime Magazine*, July 18, 2019, https://cybersecurityventures.com/how-many-internet-users-will-the-world-have-in-2022-and-in-2030/ (Accessed November 12, 2019)

12   SINTEF, "Big Data, for Better or Worse: 90% of World's Data Generated Over Last Two Years," https://www.sintef.no/en/publications/publication/?pubid=CRIStin+1031676 (Accessed November 12, 2019)

13   "10 Key Marketing Trends for 2017," IBM, https://paulwriter.com/10-key-marketing-trends-2017/ (Accessed March 24, 2018)

14   Ellie Polack, "New Cigna Study Reveals Loneliness at Epidemic Levels in America," Cigna, May 1, 2018, https://www.cigna.com/newsroom/news-releases/2018/new-cigna-study-reveals-loneliness-at-epidemic-levels-in-america (Accessed May 24, 2018)

15   Eric Metaxas and Stan Guthrie, "The Pandemic of Loneliness," Breakpoint, May 24, 2018, https://breakpoint.org/breakpoint-pandemic-loneliness/

16   Eric Metaxas, "Saving Truth in a Post-Truth World," Breakpoint, October 12, 2018

17 "12 Demographic & Technology Trends Changing the Nonprofit Sector Worldwide," Nonprofit Tech For Good, September 3, 2017, http://www.nptechforgood.com/2017/09/03/12-demographic-technology-trends-changing-the-nonprofit-sector-worldwide/

18 Rohit Arora, "The American dream is still alive: Survey," CNBC, April 15, 2016, https://www.cnbc.com/2016/04/14/rise-of-minority-businesses-in-the-us-survey.html

19 "World Report on Disability," World Health Organization, http://www.who.int/disabilities/world_report/2011/report/en/

20 Tiffany Kary, "Corporate America Can't Afford to Ignore Gen Z," Bloomberg, March 29, 2019, https://www.bloomberg.com/news/articles/2019-03-29/how-gen-z-s-different-than-millennials-companies-try-asmr-memes (Accessed November 15, 2019)

21 In 2018, women and minorities held 34 percent of board seats on Fortune 500 companies, a 3 percent increase since 2016, according a report by Deloitte for the Alliance for Board Diversity.

22 "Freelancing in America: 2019," by Upwork, published on LinkedIn SlideShare on September 23, 2019. These stats were taken from Slide 4. https://www.slideshare.net/upwork/freelancing-in-america-2019?qid=1d5133d3-6fd7-44cd-b153-7c90766dfc43&v=&b=&from_search=2 (Accessed November 12, 2019)

23 "Global Talent Trends 2019: Connectivity in the Human Age," Mercer, https://www.mercer.com/content/dam/mercer/attachments/private/gl-2019-global-talent-trends-study.pdf (Accessed November 12, 2019)

24 Maslow believed humans are motivated to achieve a series of needs—physiological, first, followed by safety, love and belonging, esteem, and self-actualization.

25 Jason Bloomberg, "IBM Bets Company On Exponential Innovation In AI, Blockchain, And Quantum Computing," Forbes, March 22, 2018, https://www.forbes.com/sites/jasonbloomberg/2018/03/22/ibm-bets-company-on-exponential-innovation-in-ai-blockchain-and-quantum-computing/#263a98fb3ea2 (Accessed December 31, 2019)

26 Bloomberg, "IBM Bets Company On Exponential Innovation In AI, Blockchain, And Quantum Computing"

27 Eli Rosenberg, "The troubling case of the young Japanese reporter who worked herself to death," The Washington Post, October 5, 2017, https://www.washingtonpost.com/news/worldviews/wp/2017/10/05/the-troubling-case-of-the-young-japanese-reporter-who-worked-herself-to-death/ (Accessed April 20, 2020)

28 Dr. Stephanie Brown, "Society's self-destructive addiction to faster living," The New York Post, January 4, 2014, https://nypost.com/2014/01/04/societys-addiction-to-faster-living-is-destroying-us-doctor/ (Accessed March 24, 2018)

29 Maya Angelou, Letter to My Daughter (Random House, 2009)

30 "World Economic Outlook: Crisis and Recovery," The International Monetary Fund, April 2009, www.imf.org/external/pubs/ft/weo/2009/01/pdf/text.pdf (Accessed November 4, 2015)

31 Jonathan Karp and Anton Troianovski, "Warehouse Owner Prologis Hits a Wall; CEO Quits," The Wall Street Journal, November 13, 2008, www.wsj.com/articles/SB122651171540121229 (Accessed October 8, 2015)

32   Edmund Burke, *A Philosophical Inquiry into the Origin of Our Ideas of the Sublime and Beautiful* (Simon & Brown, 2013)

33   Roger Jones, "What CEOs Are Afraid Of," *Harvard Business Review*, February 24, 2015, hbr.org/2015/02/what-ceos-are-afraid-of (Accessed October 13, 2015)

34   Jones, "What CEOs Are Afraid Of"

35   Manfred F.R. Kets de Vries, "The Dangers of Feeling Like a Fake," *Harvard Business Review*, September 2005

36   de Vries, "The Dangers of Feeling Like a Fake"

37   de Vries, "The Dangers of Feeling Like a Fake"

38   Stephanie Vozza, "Four Things To Do When Your Team Is Smarter Than You," *Fast Company*, March 24, 2016, http://www.fastcompany.com/3058080/four-things-to-do-when-your-teams-smarter-than-you (Accessed March 24, 2016)

39   Alison Wood Brooks, Francesca Gino, and Maurice E. Schweitzer, "Smart People Ask for (My) Advice: Seeking Advice Boosts Perceptions of Competence," *Management Science* 61, no. 6 (2015). 1421-1435.

40   Vozza, "Four Things To Do When Your Team Is Smarter Than You"

41   C.S. Lewis, *Mere Christianity* (HarperOne, 2015)

42   Guy Winch, "The Key Difference Between Pride and Arrogance: Why you can gain confidence without becoming conceited," *Psychology Today*, July 29, 2014, https://www.psychologytoday.com/blog/the-squeaky-wheel/201407/the-key-difference-between-pride-and-arrogance (Accessed November 6, 2017)

43   William Wilberforce, *Practical View of the Prevailing Religious System of Professed Christians in the Higher and Middle Classes in this Country, Contrasted with Real Christianity* (Adamant Media Corporation, 2001)

44   David Brooks, "The Moral Bucket List," *The New York Times*, April 11, 2015, https://nyti.ms/1IUsWxY (Accessed April 13, 2015)

45   Bill Treasurer, "The leadership killer," SmartBrief, November 16, 2017, https://www.smartbrief.com/original/2017/11/leadership-killer (Accessed January 5, 2018)

46   Rob Copeland, "Martin Shkreli Says Drug-Price Hikes Led to Arrest," *The Wall Street Journal*, December 21, 2015, https://www.wsj.com/articles/martin-shkreli-says-drug-price-hikes-led-to-arrest-1450671884 (Accessed May 15, 2018)

47   Shkreli later was convicted of securities fraud and sentenced to seven years in federal prison.

48   Matthew Rogerson, "'Arrogant' FIFA brought crisis on itself, says former advisor," Goal, October 22, 2015, www.goal.com/en/news/745/fifa/2015/10/22/16576762/arrogant-fifa-brought-crisis-on-itself-says-former-advisor (Accessed October 27, 2015)

49   *The MacArthur Study Bible*, commentary note on Psalm 131

50 Chris Wright, "Why Volkswagen's Attitude May Make Its Share Price Problems A Whole Lot Worse," *Forbes*, October 14, 2015, https://www.forbes.com/sites/chriswright/2015/10/14/why-volkswagens-attitude-may-make-its-share-price-problems-a-whole-lot-worse/#4e1561e5e783 (Accessed October 27, 2015)

51 J.R.R. Tolkien, *The Fellowship of the Ring* (George Allen & Unwin, 1954)

52 From "Distichs" in *The Poems of Goethe* (1853) as translated by Edgar Alfred Bowring

53 "Homeless Prisoner Gets 3 to 6 years, Victim Losing Eye," *Pittsburgh Post-Gazette*, July 13, 1960

54 H.P. Lovecraft, "Supernatural Horror in Literature," *The Recluse Magazine*, 1927

55 AON Management Consulting, *Rath & Strong's Six Sigma Leadership Handbook* (Wiley, 2003), 480

56 David Rock, "Managing with the Brain in Mind," strategy+business, Autumn 2009, Issue 56, www.strategy-business.com/article/09306?gko=5df7f (Accessed November 13, 2015)

57 Nelson Mandela, *Long Walk to Freedom* (Back Bay Books, 1995)

58 Nelson Mandela (address, Cape Town, South Africa, February 11, 1990)

59 Howard Schultz, in an interview with Oprah Winfrey, 2013

60 Sources for this story included: whc.unesco.org/en/list/637, en.wikipedia.org/wiki/Jiuzhaigou, jiuzhai.com/language/english/, and jiuzhai.com/language/english/info_legend.html

61 Sources for this story included: wikipedia.org/wiki/Onondaga_Lake, haudenosauneeconfederacy.com/influenceondemocracy.html, onondaganation.org/land-rights/onondaga-lake/, and Syracuse.com

62 Ray Williams, "Why Every CEO Needs a Coach," *Psychology Today*, posted August 13, 2012 (Accessed June 9, 2016) (Note: the article no longer is available on *Psychology Today*'s website, but it can be found at www.mkrecoverycoaching.com/2012/08/17/why-every-ceo-needs-a-coach/ [Accessed April 21, 2020]; an updated version is on Williams' website at https://raywilliams.ca/)

63 Williams, "Why Every CEO Needs a Coach"

64 Charles Caleb Colton, *Lacon* (Longman, Hurst, Rees, Orme, and Brown, 1820)

65 "Morgan Stanley Announces CEO Succession Plan," September 10, 2009, www.morganstanley.com/about-us-articles/ad3bec19-9e49-11de-b417-0db96b986471.html (Accessed October 9, 2015)

66 Curt Coffman and Kathie Sorensen, *Culture Eats Strategy for Lunch* (Liang Addison Press, 2013)

67 John Adams and Abigail Adams, *The Letters of John and Abigail Adams* (Penguin Classics, 2003)

68 According to Wikiquote, this was an inscription quoting Lincoln in an English college in *The Baptist Teacher for Sunday-school Workers*, vol. 36 (1905), 483.

69 There's debate among scholars as to whether Lincoln actually said this. James Cornelius, writing for *The Daily Beast*, traces it to an article by Noah Brooks, who attributed it to Lincoln in an 1865 article for *Harper's Weekly* a few months after Lincoln's death.

70 "The Wizard's wisdom: 'Woodenisms,'" ESPN, June 4, 2010, https://www.espn.com/mens-college-basketball/news/story?id=5249709 (Accessed November 13, 2019)

71 The quotes and most of the background for this illustration came from, "This CEO is helping Saudi women break a gender barrier," by Erika Fry, *Fortune*, September 14, 2015.

72 Stephen Wright and Eileen Ng, "AirAsia boss applies deft touch in crash response," *The Seattle Times*, January 3, 2015, https://www.seattletimes.com/business/airasia-boss-applies-deft-touch-in-crash-response/ (Accessed April 20, 2020)

73 Wright and Ng, "AirAsia boss applies deft touch in crash response"

74 CNBC.com staff, "AirAsia boss: Southeast Asia needs to fix this," CNBC, September 9, 2015, https://www.cnbc.com/2015/09/09/tony-fernandes-calls-out-southeast-asian-leaders.html (Accessed November 13, 2019)

75 Joe Torre and Tom Verducci, *The Yankee Years* (Anchor, 2010)

76 Torre and Verducci, *The Yankee Years*

77 Ralph Waldo Emerson, "Essays (On Prudence)"

78 Luke 4:11

79 John Wooden, *They Call Me Coach* (Word Books, 1972)

80 Ronald E. Riggio, "The Leadership of John Wooden," *Psychology Today*, June 5, 2010, www.psychologytoday.com/blog/cutting-edge-leadership/201006/the-leadership-john-wooden (Accessed December 16, 2015)

81 Riggio, "The Leadership of John Wooden"

82 Widely quoted in books of quotes and on websites of quotes, e.g., *Treasury of Spiritual Wisdom: A Collection of 10,000 Inspirational Quotations* by Andy Zubko, but the original source is unclear.

83 Thomas Moore, *The Poetical Works of Thomas Moore* (John Wurtele Lovell, 1881)

84 Thomas Merton, *No Man Is an Island* (Mariner Books, 2002)

85 Simone Weil, *Letter to a Priest* (Routledge, 2002)

86 Widely quoted on websites of quotes, e.g. www.goodreads.com, but the original source is unclear (which is also true for this Einstein quote: "I never said half the crap people said I did.")

87 Ralph Marston, "Humility," *The Daily Motivator*, August 1, 2016, http://greatday.com/motivate/160801.html (Accessed August 15, 2016)

88 David Brooks, "The Moral Bucket List," *The New York Times*, April 11, 2015, https://www.nytimes.com/2015/04/12/opinion/sunday/david-brooks-the-moral-bucket-list.html (Accessed April 13, 2015)

89   Jeanine Prime and Elizabeth Salib, "The Best Leaders Are Humble Leaders," *Harvard Business Review*, May 12, 2014, https://hbr.org/2014/05/the-best-leaders-are-humble-leaders (Accessed October 23, 2015)

90   Rick Warren, *The Purpose Driven Life* (Zondervan, 2013)

91   Christine Porath, "No Time to Be Nice," *The New York Times*, June 21, 2015, SR1

92   "The Way I Work: Paul English of Kayak," as told to Liz Welch, Inc.com, http://www.inc.com/magazine/20100201/the-way-i-work-paul-english-of-kayak.html (Accessed August 18, 2016)

93   Letter to Nathaniel Macon, from *The Writings of Thomas Jefferson: Correspondence, contin. Reports and opinions while Secretary of State* (January 12, 1819)

94   Barrett's 2014 composite survey included employees from 272 organizations around the world.

95   William Boston, Hendrik Varnholt, and Sarah Sloat, "Volkswagen Blames 'Chain of Mistakes' for Emissions Scandal," *The Wall Street Journal*, December 10, 2015, http://www.wsj.com/articles/vw-shares-up-ahead-of-emissions-findings-1449740759 (Accessed December 14, 2015)

96   Theranos.com/company (Accessed August 22, 2016, before the company shut down)

97   "Theranos, CEO Holmes, and Former President Balwani Charged With Massive Fraud," March 14, 2018, https://www.sec.gov/news/press-release/2018-41

98   "Paralympic Chief on Doping: 'Medals Over Morals Disgust Me,'" NBC News, August 7, 2016, http://www.nbcnews.com/video/paralympic-chief-on-doping-medals-over-morals-disgust-me-739734083959 (Accessed August 8, 2016)

99   "Paralympic Chief on Doping: 'Medals Over Morals Disgust Me'"

100 "Paralympic Chief on Doping: 'Medals Over Morals Disgust Me'"

101 Owen Gibson, "Russia given blanket Paralympic ban amid 'medals over morals' criticism," *The Guardian*, August 8, 2016, https://www.theguardian.com/sport/2016/aug/08/russia-blanket-paralympic-ban-medals-over-morals-rio-2016 (Accessed August 8, 2016)

102 Ryan Bradley, "The woman driving Patagonia to be (even more) radical," *Fortune*, September 14, 2015

103 "George Washington Carver," National Park Service, https://www.nps.gov/gwca/planyourvisit/upload/GWCA_S1.pdf

104 This quote is from a speech Lombardi often delivered, included the last time on June 22, 1970, in Dayton, Ohio, a few months before he died. The speech (and quote) is including in the book *Lombardi: What It Takes To Be #1* by Vince Lombardi, Jr. (McGraw Hill, 2001).

105 John Wooden, *A Game Plan for Life* (Bloomsbury USA, 2011)

106 Pat Williams, David Wimbish, and Bill Walton, *How to Be Like Coach Wooden* (Health Communications, Incorporated, 2006)

107 Williams, Wimbish, and Walton, *How to Be Like Coach Wooden*

108 Joann S. Lublin, "Companies Try a New Strategy: Empathy Training," *The Wall Street Journal*, June 21, 2016, http://www.wsj.com/articles/companies-try-a-new-strategy-empathy-1466501403 (Accessed August 8, 2016)

109 You can find this quote in several books, including *TEAM: The 17 Indisputable Lows of Teamwork* by John Maxwell. I emailed Kushner's assistant at Temple Israel of Natickin in Massachusetts, and she confirmed that he is the author of the quote.

110 Jana Gallus, "Fostering public good contributions with symbolic awards: A large-scale natural field experiment at Wikipedia," *Management Science* 63, no. 12 (2017). 3999–4015

111 George Bernard Shaw, *Man and Superman* (Penguin, 2001)

112 Winston S. Churchill, "Unemployment," (speech, Kinnaird Hall, Dundee, Scotland, October 10, 1908) in *Liberalism and the Social Problem: A Collection of Early Speeches as a Member of Parliament* (Echo Library, 2007)

113 Steve Taylor, "The Power of Purpose," *Psychology Today*, July 21, 2013, https://www.psychologytoday.com/us/blog/out-the-darkness/201307/the-power-purpose (Accessed June 5, 2018)

114 Vic Strecher, "Life On Purpose," Victor J. Strecher, 2017, https://www.vicstrecher.com/ (Accessed June 6, 2018)

115 James Hamblin, "Health Tip: Find Purpose in Life," *The Atlantic*, November 3, 2014, https://www.theatlantic.com/health/archive/2014/11/live-on-purpose/382252/ (Accessed June 11, 2018)

116 Allen Greenberg, "Millennials optimistic about job outlook," *Mundelein Community Bank*, October 30, 2017

117 Rob Asghar, "What Millennials Want In The Workplace (And Why You Should Start Giving It To Them," *Forbes*, January 13, 2014

118 Richard Fry, "Millennials surpass Gen Xers as the largest generation in the U.S. labor force," *Pew Research Center*, May 11, 2015

119 Morley Winograd and Dr. Michael Hais, "How Millennials Could Upend Wall Street and Corporate America," Governance Studies, The Brookings Institution, May 2014

120 Staff, "Generation Uphill," *The Economist*, January 21, 2016, special report, https://www.economist.com/special-report/2016/01/21/generation-uphill (Accessed April 21, 2020)

121 Meghan M. Biro, "Transparency Is the Key to Recruiting Young Talent," HuffPost Business, October 22, 2015, http://www.huffingtonpost.com/meghan-m-biro-/transparency-is-the-key-t_b_8363284.html (Accessed December 31, 2015)

122 Tracy Francis and Fernanda Hoefel, "'True Gen': Generation Z and its implications for companies," McKinsey & Company, November 2018, https://www.mckinsey.com/industries/consumer-packaged-goods/our-insights/true-gen-generation-z-and-its-implications-for-companies (Accessed January 6, 2020)

123 Michael Maccoby with Tim Scudder, *The Leaders We Need: And What Makes Us Follow (2nd Edition)* (Personal Strengths Publishing, Inc., 2018)

124 "Martin Shkreli: 'I Would've Raised Prices Higher,'" *Forbes*, December 2015, https://www.forbes.com/video/4644635141001/#5e56fb911017 (Accessed December 9, 2015)

125 David Gelles, "Marc Benioff of Salesforce: 'Are We Not All Connected?'" *The New York Times*, June 15, 2018

126 Gelles, "Marc Benioff of Salesforce: 'Are We Not All Connected?'"

127 "Three Methods Of Reform" in pamphlets (1900) as translated by Aylmer Maude

128 Warren, *The Purpose Driven Life*

129 Warren, *The Purpose Driven Life*

130 "Earth, Wind, and Fire Biography," https://www.earthwindandfire.com/history/biography/ (Accessed January 26, 2019)

131 Lillian McTernan, "The biggest heroes of Hurricane Harvey," *The List*, September 2017, https://www.thelist.com/83791/biggest-heroes-hurricane-harvey/ (Accessed January 5, 2018)

132 McTernan, "The biggest heroes of Hurricane Harvey"

133 Keely Levins, "The most meaningful win of 2017: How Stacy Lewis' selfless act for the people of Houston became a career-defining moment," *Golf Digest*, December 12, 2017

134 "From the Editors: Why J.J. Watt and Jose Altuve are SI's Sportsperson of the Year Honorees," *Sports Illustrated*, December 5, 2017

135 Tom Verducci, "SI's 2017 Sportsperson of the Year: José Altuve Defied Odds to Bring Houston Hope … and a Title," *Sports Illustrated*, December 5, 2017

136 "From the Editors: Why J.J. Watt and Jose Altuve are SI's Sportsperson of the Year Honorees"

137 Emily Higginbotham, "In *On Fire*, John O'Leary Details How Jack Buck—and Other St. Louisans—Saved His Life," *Riverfront Times*, March 22, 2016, https://www.riverfronttimes.com/artsblog/2016/03/22/in-on-fire-john-oleary-details-how-jack-buck-and-other-st-louisans-saved-his-life (Accessed June 11, 2018)

138 "John O'Leary's Keynote: The Power of One," John O'Leary Live Inspired, 2015, http://johnolearyinspires.com/jackbuck/

139 Another wonderful source about this story is the video, "MLB Network: Jack and The Kid," which is available on YouTube; it's narrated by Jack Buck's son, Joe Buck.

140 Rodgers Palmer and Bill Schaninger, "The link between meaning and organizational health," *McKinsey Quarterly*, October 2018

141 Anton Troianovski, "Warehouse Giants AMB Property, ProLogis to Merge," *The Wall Street Journal*, January 31, 2011, https://www.wsj.com/articles/SB10001424052748703 43950457611579334225946 (Accessed January 29, 2019)

142 "On the Conversations of Lords," *New Monthly Magazine*, April 1826

143 Dave Butts, (speech, The Summit, Bentonville, Arkansas, October 11, 2019)